The Gospel of Simon

Revelation of the Sacred Mysteries

Christopher Carpenter

Copyright © 2016 by Christopher Carpenter
ISBN 978-0-9887814-4-3
First Printed 2016
First Edition

All rights reserved. No part of this publication may be reproduced, copied, or transmitted in any form or by any means, electronic or mechanical, including photography, scanning, recording, or any information storage and retrieval system, without permission in writing from Christopher Carpenter.

Library of Congress Control Number: 2015919314

Printed in the United States of America
Sunshine Publishing of Clearwater
Manitou Springs, Colorado

www.SunshinePublishingOfClearwater.com

"One of the ideas that developed…was that the psychedelics…
were some sort of important hormone-like substance
which was necessary to the human race,
like the various hormones
which the body produces within its structure….
perhaps you could call them "planetary hormones"…
Healing plants are part of this category….
The ones which alter our state and perception of the universe
around us are no less important to our
development as enlightened entities
than those which heal our bodies."

Owsley Stanley, LSD Chemist

"The most compelling insight of that day was that this awesome recall had been brought about by a fraction of a gram of a white solid, but that in no way whatsoever could it be argued that these memories had been contained within the white solid. Everything I had recognized came from the depths of my memory and my psyche. I understood that our entire universe is contained in the mind and the Spirit. We may choose not to find access to it, we may even deny its existence, but it is indeed there inside us, and there are chemicals that can catalyze its availability."

Alexander "Sasha" Shulgin, Biochemist and Pharmacologist

TABLE OF CONTENTS

Preface xiii

The Gospel of Simon

    Chapter 1 - The Revelation of the Sacred Mysteries 1

    Chapter 2 - The Clear Light and Eternal Life /
        Love and Truth 1

    Chapter 3 - The Communion of Mary and Joseph 2

    Chapter 4 - The Birth of Jesus 2

    Chapter 5 - The Life of Jesus is Endangered 3
        The Visit of the Magi 3
        Flight and Return from Egypt 4

    Chapter 6 - The Baptism and Test of Jesus 5

    Chapter 7 - The Twelve Apostles 6

    Chapter 8 - On the Holy Soma / the Living Water 8
        The First Mystery 8
        The Woman at the Well 8

    Chapter 9 - On Being Born Again 9

    Chapter 10 - Ministry around Galilee 11
        Jesus Dispels an Impure Spirit 11
        On Healing Suffering 11
        The Female Disciples 12
        On the Sabbath 12

    Chapter 11 - The Sermon on the Mount 13
        The Beatitudes 13

    On the Law and the Prophets 13
    On the Light in Your Temple 14
    On Anger 14
    On Loving Your Enemies 15
    On Forgiveness 16
    On Judgment 16
    On Giving 16
    On Prayer 17
    On Living in the Moment 18
    On Your Treasures 19
    On Following Truth 19

Chapter 12 - On the Kingdom of Heaven 20
    The Parable of the Sower 20
    The Parable of the Fig Tree 21
    The Parable of the Mustard Seed 21
    The Parable of the Leaven 21
    The Parable of the Pearl 22
    The Parable of the Hidden Treasure 22
    The Parable of Treasure New and Old 22
    The Reason for Parables 22
    Within Your Temple 23

Chapter 13 - Prophets not Honored 23
    Jesus Rejected in Nazareth 23
    John Beheaded 23

Chapter 14 - On the Past 24

Chapter 15 - The Mystery of Feeding the Multitude 24

Chapter 16 - On the Living Bread / the Holy Soma 26

Chapter 17 - On the Origin of Suffering 27

Chapter 18 - On the Bread that Fills 28

TABLE OF CONTENTS

Chapter 19 - Events around Paneas 29
    The Nature of Jesus 29
    Jesus Foretells His Crucifixion 30
    The Transfiguration 30

Chapter 20 - On the Children of God 31

Chapter 21 - On Saving Lives 32

Chapter 22 - The Feast of the Tabernacles 32

Chapter 23 - The Woman Accused of Many Sins 34

Chapter 24 - The Parable of the Good Samaritan 35

Chapter 25 - On the Hypocrisy of Authorities 36
    Neglect of Love and Truth 36
    Denial of Key of Knowledge 37

Chapter 26 - On Being a Son of God 37

Chapter 27 - The Parable of the Lost Son 39

Chapter 28 - The Parable of the Workers in the Vineyard ... 40

Chapter 29 - Outside of Jerusalem 42
    On the Passion 42
    Supper with Lazarus 42

Chapter 30 - Jesus in Jerusalem 43
    Triumphant Entry 43
    Cleaning of the Temple 44
    On the Power of Faith and Belief 45

Chapter 31 - Teachings of the Temple 46
    The Parable of the Covetous Tenants 46
    On the Separation of Spiritual and Material Worlds 47
    On Life after Death 47
    On Love 48

Chapter 32 - On the Future 49

Chapter 33 - On the Sacred Mysteries 50

Chapter 34 - The Last Supper 51

Chapter 35 - The Arrest of Jesus 54

Chapter 36 - At the Palace 56
   Jesus before the High Priest 56
   Peter's Denial of Jesus 57

Chapter 37 - Jesus before Pilate and Herod Antipas 58

Chapter 38 - The Crucifixion 60

Chapter 39 - The Burial 62

Chapter 40 - Born Again as Christ 62
   At the Sepulcher 62
   The Road to Bethel 64
   In Jerusalem 65
   At the Sea of Galilee 65
   The Ascension 67

Analysis 69

Preliminary Comments 69

Evolution of Early Christianity 70

The Sacramental Use of an Entheogenic Substance -
the Holy Soma: 72
   The Visit of the Magi 76
   Soma 77
   The Clear Light and Rebirth 79

Divinity for All the Children of God 81

TABLE OF CONTENTS

    Equality of Women 84

    The Rehabilitation/Elevation of Simon Peter 88

    The Role of Judas 92

    Jesus, the Savior - Sin vs. Suffering 93

    The Naked Man 94

    Who is Simon? 95

    Simon of Gitta 97

    Date of *The Gospel of Simon* 100

    Conclusions 101

Exhibit 1 - Forged Inscription 102

Exhibit 2 - Interpretation of Forged Inscription 103

Reference Notes 105

Bibliography 115

PREFACE

In December 1945, following the deadliest conflict in world history, the greatest horror of which was the genocide of persons of the Jewish faith, a young Muslim discovered a treasure trove of religious and historical documents that would provide new insight into the early days of Christianity. Thirteen papyrus codices comprised of fifty two treatises, written in Coptic, sealed in an earthen jar, buried around limestone caves near the city of Nag Hammadi in Upper Egypt.[1]

The text and scrolls, dating back to the third and fourth centuries, came to be known as *The Nag Hammadi Library*, a collection of mostly Gnostic writings. It is generally agreed that the Coptic texts were translated from earlier Greek sources dating back to the first and second century.[2] *The Gospel of Thomas*, heretofore the best known of the texts, has been dated to as early as AD 40 to AD 140, based on other surviving fragmentary texts, around the time or earlier than when the accepted gospels of the *New Testament* were written.[3]

The first texts of the library became publicly known through sale on the shadowy antiquities market.[4] Once the extent of the collection was known, a team was established to translate the entire body. It took over 30 years for the entire collection to be translated and published.[5] Few scholars were capable of translating these texts from the nearly extinct Coptic language, compounding the difficulty of the task.

Translation was further complicated by words that had multiple meanings and subtle nuances. The translator's themselves were limited by their own cultural expectations and conditioned beliefs.

The *Dead Sea Scrolls*, a collection of about 900 documents were discovered shortly after *The Nag Hammadi Library*. Written in Aramaic, Hebrew, and Greek, the parchment and papyrus documents date to around 150 BC to AD 70.[6] These documents shed light on the culture, beliefs, and times that gave birth to

Christianity.[7] [8] These documents also came to light initially through sale on the "grey" antiquities market.[9]

John Marco Allegro was a member of the team formed to translate the *Dead Sea Scrolls*.[10] Allegro, a scholar and philologist soon found himself in conflict with other members of the team, especially the Catholic priests, when his interpretations suggested that some of the beliefs and practices described in the scrolls were essentially Christian in nature.[11] His work challenged the belief that the *New Testament* gospels were the sole legitimate source of truth regarding the Ministry of Jesus.[12]

Allegro experienced the full wrath of the orthodox establishment when he published *The Sacred Mushroom and the Cross*.[13] [14] Allegro's analysis of biblical words and phrases, compared to the root Sumerian language, disclosed a common theme in Judaic and Christian religious practices, notably that their foundations were rooted in fertility cults that utilized entheogenic substances, the mushroom Amanita Muscaria in particular, to induce communion with God.[15] Further, when they committed these practices to writing, they would use coded language to keep their secrets hidden from unaccepting or persecuting authorities.[16]

Although Allegro's professional reputation was significantly damaged as a result of publication of *The Sacred Mushroom and the Cross*, its release stands as a landmark advancement in the knowledge of early Christianity.[17] More recently scholarly efforts have come to acknowledge the truths in his work.[18] [19]

Fortunately, in this day and time, it is no longer possible to quash publications that are heretical to the established order, like *The Sacred Mushroom and the Cross*. This is in stark contrast to the times of the *Dead Sea Scrolls* and the texts of *The Nag Hammadi Library*, when those with heretical views risked persecution and destruction of their holy documents.[20]

It was for this very real risk that the *Dead Sea Scrolls* and the texts of *The Nag Hammadi Library* were buried: to keep them safe and secure for a future time when they could be read without the fear of persecution.[21]

In the early days of Christianity, many different sects flourished, with widely disparate beliefs and practices.[22] Some groups, the Gnostics in particular, maintained that there were secret teachings of Jesus and a hidden knowledge that was not widespread.[23]

However, as the Christianity grew, so did the organizational power of those in positions of authority, especially bishops. With convergence of Christianity and the Roman Empire in the fourth century, persecution, excommunication, and anathema, of those with heretical beliefs and practices, became widespread.[24]

Those in positions of power decided which texts were to be accepted as canon of the *New Testament*.[25] Rejected texts were banished and destroyed. The Bishop of Alexandria ordered Christians in AD 367 to reject the hidden books and "cleanse the church from every defilement."[26] With these orders, many texts were destroyed, while others were hidden only to be found centuries later.

More recently, *The Gospel of Judas*, another Gnostic text, was found in Egypt.[27] When this document was actually discovered is murky at best, having come to light as many ancient documents do, through the notorious antiquities market, in 1983. The papyrus document, written in Coptic, has been dated to about AD 280 but it is believed to be a translation from the Greek with a timeframe of no later than AD 150 since it was specifically cited by Irenaeus arguing against Gnosticism circa AD 180. [28,29,30]

Now we have *The Gospel of Simon*. The gospel first came to the attention of the editor with the purchase, through a used book dealer, of a first printed edition (1970) of *The Sacred Mushroom and the Cross* (published in England). Upon initial examination, a cryptic inscription was discovered on the back cover page, attributed to a John M. Allegro, dated "8/3/72" (see Exhibit 1 for a copy). The inscription is hardly legible, but an interpretation, with assistance of others, has been attempted (see Exhibit 2).

An even greater surprise was hidden in the book cover itself: a disk with a document, *The Gospel of Simon*, written in English with interpretive notes indicating it had been translated from an earlier Greek text, the subject of which contains various surprises about the Ministry of Jesus; most significantly, the revelation that Jesus used entheogenic substances (referred to as the Holy Soma) to achieve communion with God and the Kingdom of Heaven.

The origins of the cited copy of *The Sacred Mushroom and the Cross* as well as *The Gospel of Simon* hidden therein are not known. From what has been translated from the cryptic inscription note, it appears to have been written at night, in a car, during a police stop, likely contributing to the illegibility of the writing.

It has been ascertained by the editor from reliable sources that the inscription note and signature of a John M. Allegro is not that of the John M. Allegro who wrote *The Sacred Mushroom and the Cross* – thus it is believed to be a forgery as far as attribution to the eminent scholar. Nevertheless, it leaves unanswered what was being communicated and what relationship it has, if any, to *The Gospel of Simon*.

Why were they stopped by the police? Who were they? Where were they? Were they under the influence of some entheogen? What were they trying to say? Why was *The Gospel of Simon* hidden? Was this an attempt to suppress *The Gospel of Simon*?

Although attributed as an ancient text in the discovered notes, there is no concrete evidence that *The Gospel of Simon* is truly a work of early Christianity. Clearly the author has cited many of the stories and sayings contained not only in the *New Testament* gospels, but some Gnostic works as well. So, for the most part, the text is representative of early Christian works with the exception, primarily, of its entheogenic implications. With publication of *The Gospel of Simon*, hopefully those with knowledge of its origin will come forth with explanation and evidence to answer these questions. But this text raises a much larger question than what is its origin. More important, what truth does *The Gospel of Simon* hold? Does *The Gospel of Simon* reveal the coded secret entheogenic origins of early Christianity that John Marco Allegro contended?

Following the text of *The Gospel of Simon*, an analysis of the subject matter may be found. The conclusion that the vast majority of the text is consistent with sources of early Christianity or sources that in fact pre-date Christianity is inescapable. Whether a product of early Christianity, an overactive imagination, or the divine revelation of holy secrets, *The Gospel of Simon* will challenge and stimulate your thoughts and beliefs.

THE GOSPEL OF SIMON

CHAPTER 1
THE REVELATION OF THE
SACRED MYSTERIES

1   I, Simon, by Divine Grace, have taken up this task to reveal the Truth, as seen and told by those who witnessed the events of the Age. Joyful thanks to my fellow disciples, especially James, Thomas, Mary, Matthew, Mark, Luke, and Philip, for assisting me in this endeavor.

2   As a Disciple of Truth, it is now the time to reveal the Sacred Mysteries to all peoples in all nations. Some have argued to keep them hidden, the time still not right; but the Children of God are ready to receive the ripened Holy Fruit.

3   If having acted prematurely to reveal the Mysteries of Heaven, pray the Heavenly Father will forgive this act through His Divine Providence.

CHAPTER 2
THE CLEAR LIGHT AND ETERNAL LIFE /
LOVE AND TRUTH

1   In the beginning was God: the Creator. In God was Truth, the Word in the Clear Light: Christ.

2   All things were made by the Holy One: God, the Lord of Creation; through the power of the Holy Spirit.

3   The Living Father's Flesh and Blood, the Holy Soma, brings the Truth through the Holy Spirit: In God is Eternal Life.

4   Through the Clear Light men see Eternal Life in all Creation. The Clear Light shines in darkness and darkness vanishes when the Clear Light illuminates, as ignorance vanishes when Truth

illuminates. There is a Divine Light which illuminates the Kingdom of Heaven in every man that comes into the world.

5   The Son of Man came into the world to testify to the Truth. As many as received him, he anointed them with the Holy Soma to become the Children of God, as well as them that follow Truth: which were born, not of blood, nor of the will of the flesh, nor of the will of man, but of Spirit, as Christ.

6   The Truth is in Flesh and dwells amongst us. We behold Heaven's Glory in the Clear Light.

7   Love and Truth have been revealed by Jesus, the Son of Man: deliverer of the Holy Soma.

CHAPTER 3
THE COMMUNION OF MARY AND JOSEPH

1   Mary was with child when she had yet to marry a carpenter called Joseph. He, being a good man and not wanting disgrace, was thinking of taking her from Nazareth and moving away.

2   Mary and Joseph prayed to the Living Father in Heaven for counsel, communing with the Holy Soma for answers. While they meditated on these things, an Angel of God appeared to them in a Heavenly Vision, saying to them, "Joseph, fear not to take Mary as your wife; for that which is conceived will be born of the Holy Spirit. You shall have a son and call him Jesus. He will free people and be called the Son of Man."

3   Mary then said "Be it according to Divine Grace." The Angel then disappeared. Joseph then proceeded to take Mary as his wife.

CHAPTER 4
THE BIRTH OF JESUS

1   Mary and Joseph then moved to the city of David, called Bethlehem, because they were of the house and lineage of David.

2   While they were there, Mary delivered the child, the first of her children, in a manger. The child was wrapped in swaddling clothes and named Jesus.

3   In the country, there were shepherds in the field, keeping watch over their flock by night. To keep them mindful of the Holy One during the long night, the shepherds communed with the Holy Soma.

4   As they communed, an Angel appeared to them in a Heavenly Vision. The Glory of the Heavenly Father shone all around. The Angel said to them, "I bring you good tidings of great joy, which shall be for all people: for born this day in the city of David is a Son of the Living Father. He will free people with his deliverance. This shall be a sign to you; you shall find the child wrapped in swaddling clothes, lying in a manger."

5   Suddenly there with the Angel was a multitude of Heavenly Beings praising God, saying, "Glory to God in the highest; peace on earth and good will toward men."

6   When the Angels had disappeared, the shepherds said one to another, "Let us go to Bethlehem and see this thing that has come to pass." The Heavenly Shepherd guided them and they found the child in a manger.

7   The shepherds returned, glorifying and praising God for all the things that they had heard and seen, making it known to all who would listen. All that heard it were astonished at those things that were told to them by the shepherds.

CHAPTER 5
THE LIFE OF JESUS IS ENDANGERED: THE VISIT OF THE MAGI

1   When Jesus was born, Magi from the east came to Jerusalem saying, "Where is he that will be King? For this is his Age and we have seen the great glow of his Heavenly Star; we have come

to honor him." The disciples of Zoroaster had communed with the Holy Soma, that they call Haoma.

2   When Herod the First heard these things, he was concerned that his throne might be threatened. When the king had gathered the chief priests and scribes together, he demanded to know where this child would be born.

3   They said to him, "In Bethlehem of Judea, for it is written by the prophet: *And thou Bethlehem, in the land of Judea, although small amongst the many, out of thee shall a King come for My people.*"

4   Herod then called the Magi and told them that the child was in Bethlehem, saying with ill intent, "Go and search diligently for the young child. When you have found him, bring me word again, that I may come and honor him also."

5   After meeting with Herod, they departed for Bethlehem. The Heavenly Shepherd guided them to Jesus. When they saw the child with Mary, they fell down to honor him: presenting him gifts of gold, frankincense, and myrrh.

6   Mary, Joseph, and the Magi communed in celebration with the Holy Soma. Then, an Angel appeared to them in a Heavenly Vision, saying "Arise! Move to Egypt and stay there until you receive word that it is safe, for Herod seeks to destroy male infants."

7   The Magi knew King Herod sought the life of the child, just as those of old sought the life of Zoroaster. The Magi, knowing they should not return to Herod, departed to their own land another way.

FLIGHT AND RETURN FROM EGYPT

8   Joseph then took his family and moved to Egypt. They remained there until the death of Herod. When Herod was dead,

an Angel appeared in a Heavenly Vision to Joseph, saying, "Arise, you may return to the land of Israel: for he is dead who sought children's lives."

9   Joseph decided to return to Nazareth in Galilee, as it was well removed from Bethlehem and Jerusalem. Thus it was fulfilled which was spoken by the prophets, *"Out of Egypt I have called my son."*

CHAPTER 6
THE BAPTISM AND TEST OF JESUS

1   After many years, when the time was right, Jesus went from Nazareth to the river Jordan where people were baptized by John, called the Baptist.

2   It was John's testimony that announced the coming of the Son of Man, who would reveal the Truth about the Kingdom of Heaven. From the wilderness he prepared the straight and narrow way for the Messiah, called Christ: born of the Holy Spirit.

3   Thus, Jesus was baptized while praying and communing with the Holy Soma.

4   Then, out of the Living Water, Heaven opened and the Holy Spirit like a dove descended upon him. Illuminated with the Divine Light, a voice came from Heaven, saying, "You are my beloved Son, in whom I am well pleased."

5   Jesus being full of the Spirit had a Vision: he found himself in a wilderness, his Soul to be tested by the devil.

6   The devil first said to him, "If you be a Son of God, command this stone that it be made Bread."

7   Jesus answered, **"It is written, *Man shall not live by Bread alone, but by the Word of God.*"**

8   The devil then took him up onto a high mountain, showing him all the kingdoms of the world in a moment of time. The devil then said to him, "All this power will I give you and the glory of them. Therefore, if you worship me, all shall be yours."

9   Jesus answered, **"Get behind me, Satan; for it is written,** *You shall worship the Lord thy God, and him only shall you serve."*

10   Finally, the devil brought Jesus to Jerusalem, set him on a pinnacle of the temple and said to him, "If you are a Son of God, cast yourself down from here. For it is written, He shall give his Angels charge over you to keep you safe, and in their hands they shall bear you up, lest at any time you dash your foot against a stone."

11   Jesus answered, **"It is said,** *You shall not test the Lord thy God."*

12   The devil then departed Jesus and he was illuminated by the Clear Light; Heavenly Angels came and ministered to him; the way now revealed, he returned to Galilee with the doctrine of Love and Truth.

CHAPTER 7
THE TWELVE APOSTLES

1   Jesus began his ministry with three of his brethren: James, called the Righteous; Thomas, also called Judas; and Simon, the youngest.

2   They traveled around Galilee, Jesus teaching about the Kingdom of Heaven and healing the sick and those suffering from impure spirits amongst the poor and rich alike. Many eyes were opened and many heard the Truth.

3   Later, as they walked by the Sea of Galilee, Jesus saw four men: two brothers, James and John, the sons of Zebedee, mending

their nets; and two other brothers, Andrew and Simon: who Jesus surnamed the Stone, and called Simon Peter; casting a net into the sea; for they were all fishermen and partners. They had heard the astonishing things that were said about Jesus and heard him teach as one having authority of the Spirit and not as the scribes.

4   Jesus said to them, **"Follow me and you will become fishers of men."**

5   They left their nets and followed him.

6   Another time, as Jesus passed by the sea, he saw a publican, Levi, who collected taxes at the customs office.

7   Jesus said to him, **"Follow me and you will become a collector of men."**

8   So Levi, having heard the astonishing things said of Jesus and having heard his sermons, followed him. Thereafter Jesus called him Matthew.

9   The others that followed Jesus were: Judas; Jude; Philip; and Bartholomew.

10 When he had called unto him the twelve apostles, he began teaching them the Sacred Mysteries in order that they might heal those suffering from sickness and impure spirits.

11 Jesus told them, **"You are twelve to signify the tribes of Creation and the Children of God's struggles throughout the Ages."**

12 The disciples believed in the Truth Jesus taught.

CHAPTER 8
ON THE HOLY SOMA / THE LIVING WATER: THE FIRST MYSTERY

1   In Cana of Galilee there was the wedding of a certain young man. Many people attended the wedding. After a while, Mary said to Jesus, "There is no more wine."

2   Now there were some stone containers holding water used for ceremonial purification. In accordance with the Sacred Mysteries, Jesus anointed the empty serving water pots with the Holy Soma.

3   Jesus then said to the servants, **"Fill the water pots with the ceremonial water."** They filled them up to the brim with water. Next Jesus said to them, **"Draw out the Drink and bear unto the governor of the feast."**

4   The governor of the feast then drank the Living Water.

5   Later, the governor called the bridegroom and said to him, "Most men provide better wine first; and when they have drunk a lot, then provide that which is worse; but you have kept the Best Drink till last."

6   Thus, Jesus performed this first open act of the Mysteries, in Cana of Galilee, manifesting the power of the Spirit. His disciples believed in him; his fame spreading beyond Galilee.

THE WOMAN AT THE WELL

7   Jesus was traveling through Samaria, close to Mount Gerizim, a holy place for the Samaritans. He came to a city near the ground that Jacob gave to his son Joseph. Jacob's well was there. Jesus, being weary from his journey, sat on the well.

8   A woman of Samaria came to draw water from the well; Jesus being thirsty, asked her for drink.

9   Now the Jews and Samaritans were as enemies to one another. The woman therefore said to him, "How is it that you, being a Jew, ask drink of me, a Samaritan woman?"

10   Jesus answered, **"If you knew the Sacramental Gift of God and who it is that asked you for drink; you would have asked him for drink and he would have given you Living Water."**

11   The woman said to him, "Sir, you have nothing to draw with and the well is deep. From where will you get this Living Water? Are you greater than our father Jacob, who gave us this well and drank from it himself?"

12   Jesus answered, **"Whoever drinks of this water shall thirst again, but whoever drinks of the Water of Truth shall never thirst. The Water that I provide is a well of Living Water springing up into Eternal Life."**

13   The woman said to him, "Sir, give me this water, that I thirst not, neither come here to draw. We worship here in this mountain as our fathers did; but the Jews say that the temple in Jerusalem is the place where people ought to worship."

14   Jesus answered, **"Truly, I say to you, the hour comes when you shall worship God neither in this mountain nor in Jerusalem. The hour comes and now is, when True worshippers shall worship in Spirit and Truth, wherever their Temple may be."**

15   The woman, thus anointed with the Living Water, then believed and followed Jesus, thereafter being called Photini.

CHAPTER 9
ON BEING BORN AGAIN

1   While they were in Jerusalem for the Feast of Weeks, a man called Nicodemus came to Jesus late one night. He was a

Councilor of the Sanhedrin and of the Pharisees, who believe a Messiah will come.

2   Nicodemus said to him, "We know that you are a teacher from God, for no man can do these works that you do, except God be with him."

3   Jesus answered, **"Truly, I say to you, unless you be born again, you cannot see the Kingdom of Heaven."**

4   Nicodemus said to him, "How can a man be born when he is old? Can he enter his mother's womb a second time and be born?"

5   Jesus answered, **"Unless you be born of the Spirit as Christ, you cannot enter the Kingdom of Heaven. That which is born of the flesh is flesh; and that which is born of the Spirit is Spirit.**

6   **The Holy Soma will open your eyes with the Clear Light; you must die to be born again, but Eternal Life comes with death. For every end is a beginning. Marvel not that I said you must be born again.**

7   **The wind blows where it pleases, and you hear the sound thereof, but cannot tell when it comes and where it goes. So it is with everyone that is born of the Spirit. No eye of an Angel has ever seen it. No thought of man's heart has fully comprehended it. No hand has ever touched it."**

8   Nicodemus asked, "How can these things be?"

9   Jesus answered, **"How is it that you, a master of Israel, not know these things? If I have told you earthly things and you do not believe, how shall you believe if I tell you of Heavenly things? Whoever follows Truth will not perish, but have Eternal Life."**

CHAPTER 10
MINISTRY AROUND GALILEE:
JESUS DISPELS AN IMPURE SPIRIT

1   Jesus and the disciples went into Capernaum. On the Sabbath day he entered into the synagogue and taught. The people were astonished at his doctrine; for he taught them as one having authority of the Spirit and not as the scribes.

2   There was a man in the synagogue that was being tested, suffering the fire of an impure spirit. He cried out, saying, "Let us alone; what have we to do with you, Jesus of Nazareth? We know you are a Light of God, the Holy One."

3   Jesus dispelled the impure spirit, guiding him, saying, **"Find your peace and let the Living Water cleanse your Soul."**

4   The fire was thus quenched and the impure spirit left him; he cried with relief, as Jesus saved him from his suffering.

5   The people were astonished and they questioned amongst themselves, "What kind of magic is this? What new doctrine is this, for he commands even the bad spirits?"

6   His fame spread as he healed many more that were suffering.

ON HEALING SUFFERING

7   It came to pass that Matthew hosted a great feast in his own house. As Jesus sat to eat, many publicans and sinners came and sat down with him and his disciples. When certain Pharisees saw it, they said to his disciples, "Why does your Master eat with publicans and sinners?"

8   When Jesus heard this, he answered them, **"They that are well do not need a physician, but they that are sick do need one. I will have mercy, not sacrifice; for I have come not to**

call the righteous, but those who are suffering for want of the Truth."

THE FEMALE DISCIPLES

9 Jesus traveled through the towns and villages teaching about the Kingdom of Heaven. The twelve were with him, as were many women who, having heard the Truth, believed and followed Jesus, becoming disciples as Photini. Amongst them were Mary, the wife of Cleopas; Joanna, the wife of Chuza, Herod's household manager; Susanna; and Mary Magdalene, his beloved disciple. They provided support to Jesus and the apostles from their own means.

10 Now Mary Magdalene often walked with Jesus as his companion. Some of the twelve, especially Simon Peter, were jealous of Mary's relationship with Jesus, as she was much loved. But others, like Matthew, defended Mary, saying, "If our Master believes she is worthy, who are we to reject her?"

ON THE SABBATH

11 Another week Jesus and his disciples went through corn fields on the Sabbath day and being hungry they plucked ears of corn. Now the Pharisees, who interpret the Law of Moses, saw what they had done. Certain Pharisees then said to Jesus, "Why do you do that which is not lawful on the Sabbath day?"

12 Jesus answered, **"Have you not read what David and they that were with him did when they had need and were hungry? How they went into the house of God and ate the Living Bread, which is not lawful to eat but for the priests? Truly, I say to you, the Sabbath was made for man, not man for the Sabbath."**

13 When the chief priests and scribes heard of this doctrine, they were offended and started to become fearful of what Jesus taught.

CHAPTER 11
THE SERMON ON THE MOUNT:
THE BEATITUDES

1 A great multitude of people came to Jesus from Galilee, Judea, Decapolis, and beyond the river Jordan. Seeing the people, he went up onto a mount near Capernaum. Jesus taught them the doctrine of Love and Truth, saying:

2 **"Blessed are the humble; for theirs is the Kingdom of God.**

3 **Blessed are the pure in heart; for they shall see God.**

4 **Blessed are the gentle; for they shall inherit the earth.**

5 **Blessed are they that mourn; for they shall be comforted.**

6 **Blessed are the merciful; for they shall obtain mercy.**

7 **Blessed are they that hunger and thirst after righteousness; for they shall be filled.**

8 **Blessed are the peacemakers; for they shall be called the Children of God.**

9 **Blessed are they which are persecuted for the Holy Soma; for theirs is the Kingdom of Heaven.**

10 **Blessed are you, when men shall revile you, persecute you, and say all manner of evil against you. Rejoice and be exceedingly glad; for great is your reward in Heaven; for so persecuted were the prophets before you.**

ON THE LAW AND THE PROPHETS

11 **Think not that I have come to destroy the law or the prophets. I have not come to destroy, but to fulfill. Until Heaven and earth pass, not one letter shall pass from the law.**

12 Therefore, whoever shall break the least of the commandments and teach men to do so, he shall be called the least in the Kingdom of Heaven. But whoever shall do and teach them, the same shall be called great in the Kingdom of Heaven.

13 Love others as yourself. Therefore in all things, do unto others as you would have them do unto you.

14 This is the law and the prophets.

ON THE LIGHT IN YOUR TEMPLE

15 Your body is a Temple for the Soul. The Light of your Temple is the eye. If therefore your eye be clear, your Temple shall be full of Clear Light. But if your eye be bad, your temple shall be in darkness. If therefore the light that is in you be darkness, how great is that darkness!

16 You are the Light of the world. A city that is set on a hill cannot be hid; neither do men light a candle and put it under a cover, but on a candlestick; and it gives Light to all that are in the house. Let your Light shine before men, that they may see your good and glorify the Kingdom of Heaven.

ON ANGER

17 You have heard it said by them of old, *You shall not kill; and whoever kills shall be in danger of judgment.*

18 But I say to you that whoever is angry with his brother shall be in danger of judgment.

19 Therefore if you bring a gift to the altar and there remember that your brother has fought against you; leave the gift before the altar and go your way. First be reconciled with your brother; then come and offer the gift.

20 Agree with your adversary quickly, while you are with him; lest at any time the adversary deliver you to the judge, and the judge deliver you to the officer, and you be cast into prison. You shall by no means get out until you have paid all that you owe.

ON LOVING YOUR ENEMIES

21 You have heard it said: *An eye for an eye and a tooth for a tooth*.

22 But I say to you, resist not evil. Whoever strikes you on your right cheek, turn to him the other also.

23 And if any man sues you at the law and takes away your coat, let him have your overcoat also.

24 And whoever compels you to go a mile, go with him two.

25 Give to him that ask you and from him that would borrow from you do not turn away.

26 You have heard it said, *You shall Love your neighbor and hate your enemy*. But I say to you, Love your enemy as your neighbor. Bless them that curse you, do good to them that hate you, and pray for them which despitefully use you and persecute you; that you may be the Children of your Heavenly Father.

27 For the Lord of Creation makes the sun rise on the evil and on the good; and sends rain on the just and on the unjust. For if you love them which love you, what reward have you? Do not even the Gentiles do the same? And if you salute your brethren only, what more do you do than others? Do not even the Gentiles do the same? Be therefore perfect as your Father in Heaven is perfect.

ON FORGIVENESS

28 If you forgive men their trespasses, your Heavenly Father will also forgive you. But if you do not forgive men their trespasses, neither will your Living Father forgive your trespasses.

ON JUDGMENT

29 Judge not, lest you be judged. For with what judgment you judge, you shall be judged: and with what measure you give, it shall be measured to you again.

30 Why behold the speck that is in your brother's eye, but consider not the beam that is in your own eye? Or how will you say to your brother, Let me pull the speck out of your eye, when a beam is in your own eye? You hypocrite, first cast the beam out of your own eye; then you shall see clearly to cast the speck out of your brother's eye.

ON GIVING

31 Take heed that you do not give your donations to be seen by men; otherwise you have no reward in Heaven.

32 Therefore when you give, do not sound a trumpet before you, as the hypocrites do in the synagogues and in the streets, that they may have glory of men. Truly, I say to you, they have their reward.

33 But when you give, do not let your left hand know what your right hand does, that your donations may be in secret. Truly, I say to you, what your Father sees in secret, he shall reward openly.

ON PRAYER

34 When you pray, be not as the hypocrites. For they love to pray standing in the synagogues and on the corners of the streets, that they may be seen. Truly, I say to you, they have their reward.

35 But when you pray, enter into your closet and shut the door. Pray to your Heavenly Father in secret with faith and belief. Truly, I say to you, what your Father sees in secret, he shall reward openly.

36 When you pray, use not vain repetitions, as the Gentiles do. For they think that they shall be heard for their much speaking. Be not like them, for your Living Father knows what things you need before you ask.

37 So, ask and it shall be given to you. Seek and you shall find. Knock and it shall be opened to you. For every one that asks, receives; and he that seeks, finds; and to him that knocks, it shall be opened.

38 What man is there amongst you, whom if his son asks for bread, will give him a stone? Or if he asks for a fish, will give him a snake?

39 If you then, being evil, know how to give good gifts to your children, how much more shall your Heavenly Father give good things to them that ask?

40 Therefore, pray like this:

>   Our Father which is in Heaven:
>   Hallowed be your name;
>   Your Kingdom come;
>   Your Will be done,
>   on earth as in Heaven;
>   Give us this day our Living Bread;

And forgive us our debts,
as we forgive our debtors;
And lead us not into temptation; but
Deliver us from evil.
Amen.

ON LIVING IN THE MOMENT

41 Be not anxious for your Life, what you shall eat, what you shall drink; nor yet for your body, what you shall wear. Is not Life more than food and the body more than clothing?

42 Behold the birds of the air: they do not sow; neither do they reap, nor gather into barns; yet your Heavenly Father feeds and provides for them. Are you not much better than they?

43 Which of you by being anxious can add one moment to your lifespan?

44 Why be anxious about clothing? Consider the lilies of the field, how they grow; they toil not, neither do they spin. Yet I say to you, even Solomon in all his glory was not arrayed like one of these. Therefore, if God so clothes the grass of the field, which today is and tomorrow is not, shall He not much more clothe you?

45 Therefore be not anxious, saying, What shall we eat? Or, what shall we drink? Or, how shall we be clothed? For your Heavenly Father knows that you have need of all these things.

46 But first seek the Kingdom of Heaven with Love and Truth; then all things will be provided by the power of the Spirit; Creation itself shall be revealed to you in a moment of Divine Grace.

47 Therefore, be not anxious for tomorrow: for tomorrow shall be anxious for the things of itself. Sufficient unto the day are the troubles thereof.

ON YOUR TREASURES

48 Do not give that which is Holy to the dogs; neither cast your Pearls before swine, lest they trample them under their feet, then turn again and rend you.

49 No man can serve two masters. For either he will hate the one and love the other; or else he will hold to the one and despise the other. Nor can a man mount two horses or stretch two bows. You cannot serve both God and earthly treasures.

50 Do not store your Treasures upon the earth, where moth and rust corrupts; where thieves break in and steal. But store your Treasures in Heaven, where neither moth nor rust corrupts; where thieves do not break in and steal. For where your Treasure is, there will be your heart also.

ON FOLLOWING TRUTH

51 Enter in at the strait gate. For wide is the gate and broad is the way that leads to destruction; many go that way. Strait is the gate and narrow is the way that leads to Truth and Eternal Life; few find it.

52 Beware of those bearing falsehoods that come to you in sheep's clothing, but inwardly are ravening wolves. You shall know them by their fruits. Do men gather grapes of thorns or figs of thistles?

53 Every good tree brings forth good Fruit; but a corrupt tree brings forth evil fruit. A good tree cannot bring forth evil fruit; neither can a corrupt tree bring forth good fruit. Therefore by their Fruits you shall know them.

54 Not everyone that says, Lord, Lord, shall enter into the Kingdom of Heaven; but he that does the will of God in Heaven shall enter. Many will say, Lord, Lord, have we not prophesied in your name? In your name done many

wonderful works? In your name built many houses of worship? In your name taught as the apostles? And the Lord will say, I never knew you; depart from me, you that do not abide with Truth.

55 Therefore whoever hears the Truth and follows, I will liken him to a wise man, who built his house upon a rock; and the rain descended, and the floods came, and the winds blew, and beat upon that house; and it fell not, for it was founded upon stone.

56 And every one that hears the Truth and does not follow, shall be likened to a foolish man, who built his house upon sand; and the rain descended, and the floods came, and the winds blew, and beat upon that house; and it fell, and great was the fall."

57 When Jesus had ended these sayings, the people were astonished by his teachings, for he taught them as one having authority of the Spirit and not as the scribes. Hearing what Jesus had spoken, many believed the Truth, becoming his disciples, spreading the Word.

CHAPTER 12
ON THE KINGDOM OF HEAVEN:
THE PARABLE OF THE SOWER

1 Another day, Jesus went to the Sea of Galilee with the disciples. A great multitude gathered together unto him, so he went onto a boat and sat. The whole multitude stood on the shore and he spoke to them of the Kingdom of Heaven.

2 "Behold, a sower went forth to sow.

3 When he sowed, some seeds fell by the way side, and the birds came and devoured them; some fell upon stony places where they had little earth, and forthwith they sprung up because they had no deepness of earth, and when the sun came

up they were scorched, and because they had no root they withered away; and some fell amongst thorns and the thorns sprung up and choked them.

4   But other seed fell into Good ground and brought forth Fruit, some a hundredfold, some sixtyfold, some thirtyfold.

5   He who has ears, let him hear.

THE PARABLE OF THE FIG TREE

6   A certain man had planted a fig tree in his vineyard. Later he came and sought fruit thereon, but found none.

7   Then he said to the keeper of his vineyard, Behold, I have come seeking fruit on this fig tree and found none. Cut it down; why let it take space in the ground?

8   And he answering said, Lord, let it alone this year, till I dig and Fertilize it. If it then bears Fruit, Good; and if not, then cut it down.

THE PARABLE OF THE MUSTARD SEED

9   The Kingdom of Heaven is like a grain of Mustard Seed, which a man took and sowed in his field. Although indeed it is the least of all seeds, when it is grown, it is great amongst herbs and becomes a Tree, providing shelter for the birds of the air in the branches thereof.

THE PARABLE OF THE LEAVEN

10 The Kingdom of Heaven is like Leaven, which a woman took and mixed in meal till the Whole was Leavened.

THE PARABLE OF THE PEARL

11 The Kingdom of Heaven is like a merchant man, seeking Good pearls, who when he had found one Pearl of great price, went and sold all that he had and bought it.

THE PARABLE OF THE HIDDEN TREASURE

12 The Kingdom of Heaven is like a Treasure hid in a field; which when a man has found, he hides, and for joy thereof goes and sells all that he has and buys that field."

THE PARABLE OF TREASURE NEW AND OLD

13 Jesus then asked them, **"Have you understood all these things?"**

14 They said to him, "Yes, Master."

15 Then he said to them, **"Therefore every scribe that is instructed in the Kingdom of Heaven is like a man that is a house owner, who brings forth out of his laid up Treasure, things new and old."**

THE REASON FOR PARABLES

16 When Jesus had finished speaking to the multitude, a certain young disciple came to Jesus asking, "Master, why do you speak to the people in parables?"

17 He answered, **"It is given to you, my disciples, to know the Sacred Mysteries of the Kingdom of Heaven, but it is not given to them at this time. Therefore I speak to them in parables; because they seeing, see not; and they hearing, hear not; they do not understand.**

18 **But blessed are you: for you were blind and now you see; you were deaf and now you hear. Many prophets and**

righteous people have desired to see those things which you see, but have not seen them; and to hear those things which you hear, but have not heard them."

WITHIN YOUR TEMPLE

19 Jesus was then asked when the Kingdom of Heaven would come. He answered, **"Truly I say to you, the Kingdom of Heaven comes not with observation. Neither shall they say, Look here! Or, look there! For, behold, the Kingdom of Heaven is within you."**

CHAPTER 13
PROPHETS NOT HONORED:
JESUS REJECTED IN NAZARETH

1 When Jesus had finished at the Sea of Galilee, he departed to Nazareth. He taught them in the synagogues and they were astonished, for he spoke as one having authority of the Spirit and not as the scribes.

2 They said, "How has this man this wisdom and these mighty works? Is not this the carpenter's son? Is not his mother Mary? His brothers: James, Judas, Joseph, and Simon? And his sisters: are they not all with us? How then does this man know all these things?" So they rejected him and did not recognize Truth.

3 Jesus then said to them, **"A prophet is honored everywhere except in his own hometown."**

JOHN BEHEADED

4 At this time, Herod Antipas had John the Baptist in prison; for John, who had influence with the people, had offended him. Herod feared that the doctrine taught by John and his condemnations would stir the people against him, threatening his throne; therefore, Herod had the Baptist beheaded.

5   Now the people were highly offended by Herod's act, saying God would be displeased; for the people held John to be a righteous man. Many believed that he was the prophet Elijah returned.

CHAPTER 14
ON THE PAST

1   Upon hearing of John's death, Jesus called the twelve disciples together and gave them power and authority in accordance with the Sacred Mysteries. He sent them forth to teach the Kingdom of Heaven.

2   He told them, **"Take nothing for your journey, except the clothes that you wear and your staff; neither take bread nor money for the Holy Soma.**

3   **Whatever house you enter into, abide and then depart.**

4   **Whoever will not receive Truth, when you go out of that city, shake off the very dust from your feet as a testimony against them."**

5   A disciple said to him, "Master, let me first go and bury my father."

6   Jesus answered, **"Follow Truth and let the dead bury their own dead."**

7   They thus departed and went through the towns, teaching the Truth and healing those who were suffering.

CHAPTER 15
THE MYSTERY OF FEEDING THE MULTITUDE

1   When the disciples returned, they told Jesus all that they had done. Simon Peter said, "Master, we saw one performing the

Sacred Mysteries and dispelling impure spirits; so we forbade him, because he did not follow with us."

2   Jesus said to him, **"Do not forbid him; for he that is not against us is for us."**

3   Close to the city called Bethsaida, Jesus took the disciples and went to a private desert place to commune and rest.

4   Many people followed after Jesus, for they had heard of his works and teachings. Having compassion, he received them, about five thousand, speaking to them of the Kingdom of Heaven. They were astonished by his doctrine.

5   When the day began to wear away the twelve came to him saying, "Send the multitude away so that they may go into the towns and country to find lodging and food, for we are here in this desert place."

6   But Jesus said to them, **"We should Feed them."**

7   They said, "We have only five barley loaves of bread and two fish. Should we go and buy food for all these people?"

8   He answered, instructing them what to do, **"Have them sit down so the righteousness of their Soul may be tested."**

9   Jesus and the disciples then broke the five loaves and anointed the barley bread with the Holy Soma. The disciples then distributed the Living Bread to the multitude in twelve baskets.

10   The multitude ate the Living Bread and were all filled with the Kingdom of Heaven; they hungered no more.

11   The barley fragments that remained were taken up in the twelve baskets.

12   By reason of Jesus openly performing the Mystery of feeding the multitude, many more now heard of the works and teachings

of Jesus, his fame spreading throughout Galilee, Judea, Decapolis, and beyond the river Jordan.

13 Upon hearing of Jesus feeding the multitude, the chief priests and elders became fearful that Jesus would use Soma to stir the people to sedition.

CHAPTER 16
ON THE LIVING BREAD / THE HOLY SOMA

1 The following day, Jesus and the disciples departed separately by boat on the Sea of Galilee. When the people saw neither Jesus nor his disciples, they went to Capernaum, seeking Jesus.

2 When they had found him, they said to him, "Master, we have been looking for you." Then they asked him, "What shall we do that we might do the work of God?"

3 Jesus answered, **"This is the work of the Living Father: that you Love one another and follow Truth."**

4 Jesus then said, **"Truly, I say to you, you seek me, not because you understand the Mysteries and my teachings, but because you did eat the Living Bread and were filled with the Kingdom of Heaven. Do not labor for the bread that perishes; but for the Bread of Heaven and Eternal Life, that the Son of Man gives you."**

5 They then asked him, "What sign do you show us, that we may see and believe you?"

6 Jesus said to them, **"Oh you of little faith. Your fathers ate bread and are dead. I bring the Bread of Heaven and Eternal Life. He that righteously follows Truth shall never hunger or thirst. I come, not to do my own will, but the will of Him that sends me. And this is the will of Him that sends me, that every one that follows Truth will have Eternal Life."**

7 The multitude then murmured, because he said, I bring the Bread of Heaven and Eternal Life. They asked, "What is this Bread of which he speaks? Is this not Jesus, whose father and mother we know? How is it then that he says, I bring the Bread of Heaven and Eternal Life?"

8 Jesus answered, **"Murmur not amongst yourselves. Your fathers did eat bread and are dead. The Living Bread comes from Heaven; if any man eats of this Bread, he shall be reborn to Eternal Life.**

9. **Truly, I say to you, he that follows Truth has Eternal Life. I bring the Bread of Eternal Life; the Flesh and Blood of the Lord, the Holy Soma."**

10 The multitude therefore discussed amongst them, "How can this man give us the Lord's Flesh and Blood to eat?"

11 Jesus answered, **"Truly, I say to you, whoever eats the Flesh and drinks the Blood of our Heavenly Father has Eternal Life. For the Flesh is food indeed; and the Blood is drink indeed. He that eats the Lord's Flesh and drinks the Lord's Blood, dwells in God and God in him.**

12 **This is the Bread from Heaven. Not as your fathers did eat and are dead; they that eat of the Living Bread shall never hunger, they shall see Eternal Life."**

CHAPTER 17
ON THE ORIGIN OF SUFFERING

1 Later, some Pharisees came from Jerusalem to meet Jesus. When they saw Jesus and the disciples eat bread with unwashed hands, they found fault. For Pharisees, unless they wash their hands, do not eat, holding with the tradition of old. Then certain Pharisees asked him, "Why do you not adhere to the tradition of the elders, but instead eat bread with unwashed hands?"

2   Jesus answered, **"Truly, I say to you, there is nothing from outside a man that entering into him can defile him; but the things that come out of him, that is what defiles the man. Hear and understand."**

3   The chief priests and elders, hearing of this challenge to their authority and the multitudes that now followed him, became even more fearful of the doctrine Jesus taught.

4   When he had left and entered into a house away from the people, his disciples asked him concerning the teaching.

5   He answered them, **"Are you so without understanding also? Do you not perceive that whatever thing from outside enters into the man; it cannot defile him; because it enters not into his heart, but into the belly and goes out purged?**

6   **That which comes out from within the man defiles the man. For from within, out of the heart of men, proceed impure thoughts: an evil eye, murders, assaults, thefts, covetousness, deceit, blasphemy, pride, foolishness. All these things that cause suffering come from within and defile the man.**

7   **Therefore, keep your Temple pure; then you shall see the Kingdom of Heaven."**

CHAPTER 18
ON THE BREAD THAT FILLS

1   Now the disciples had forgotten to bring bread.

2   Jesus challenged them, saying, **"Take heed, beware of the bread of the Pharisees and the bread of Herod."**

3   The disciples reasoned amongst themselves, saying, "It is because we have no bread."

4   When Jesus heard this, he asked them, **"Why do you reason because you have no bread? You do not perceive, neither do you understand. Has your heart hardened? Having eyes, do you not see? Having ears, do you not hear? Do you not remember the test of the multitude? When the five thousand were Fed with the five barley loaves? How many baskets of Living Bread fragments did you take up?"**

5   They said to him, "Twelve."

6   He asked them, **"And did the fragments not Fill you again with the Kingdom of Heaven? How many more thousands must I Feed before you understand?"**

CHAPTER 19
EVENTS AROUND PANEAS:
THE NATURE OF JESUS

1   Jesus went out with his disciples around the town of Caesarea Paneas. He asked the disciples, **"Who do the people say that I am?"**

2   A certain young disciple answered, "Some say John the Baptist, while others say Elijah. Still others say you are some other prophet that has been born again, while others say you are the Messiah, the coming King of Israel."

3   Jesus then asked them, **"And what do you say?"**

4   Simon Peter said, "You are a righteous messenger from the Lord."

5   Matthew said, "And you are a wise philosopher."

6   Thomas said, "Master, my mouth is incapable of saying who you are other than you must be a Son of God."

JESUS FORETELLS HIS CRUCIFIXION

7   He began to teach them that the Son of Man must suffer many things. He would be rejected by chief priests, elders, and scribes. He would be crucified.

8   He spoke these things to them openly. Simon Peter took him aside and began to rebuke him, saying "Be it far from you, Master. This shall not happen to you."

9   Jesus then turned about and, looking on his disciples, rebuked Simon Peter, saying, **"Get behind me, Satan; for you savor not the things of God, but the things of men. Do not be a stone upon which others stumble."**

10 Then he called the people and disciples to him, saying **"Whoever will follow me, let him deny himself and suffer on his cross. For whoever will save his life shall lose it; but whoever shall lose his life for Love and Truth, the same shall save it.**

11 **For what shall it profit a man, if he shall gain the whole world, but lose his Soul? Or what shall a man give in exchange for his Soul?"**

THE TRANSFIGURATION

12 After this, Jesus took James, John and Simon Peter, and went up onto Mount Hermon to commune with the Holy Soma. As they communed, Jesus was illuminated with the Divine Light and his clothing glowed with a luminous, white Light.

13 Jesus then communed with Moses and Elijah, who appeared in a Heavenly Vision, and contemplated the nature of man's suffering and the suffering his crucifixion would redeem.

14 Then a voice said, "This is my beloved Son, hear him," and the Angels disappeared into the clouds of Heaven.

15 As they came down from the mountain, Jesus told them to speak of these things to no one, till the Son of Man was reborn as Christ.

CHAPTER 20
ON THE CHILDREN OF GOD

1 When they came to Capernaum, Jesus talked to the people. Some of his family, his mother and brothers, stood without, calling for him. As he taught, Jesus heard from the people that sat around him, "Your mother and brothers stand without, seeking you."

2 He asked, **"Who is my mother and who are my brothers?"** He stretched forth his hand toward the people, saying, **"Behold my mother and my brothers! For whoever does the will of our Living Father in Heaven, the same is my brother, my sister, and my mother. We are the Children of God."**

3 Then a certain young disciple came to Jesus, asking, "Who is the greatest in the Kingdom of Heaven?"

4 Jesus called a little child unto him, set him in the midst of them, answering, **"Truly, I say to you, unless you be born again and become as little children, you shall not enter into the Kingdom of Heaven.**

5 **Therefore, whoever shall humble himself as this little child, the same is greatest in the Kingdom of Heaven. When you disrobe like little children and tread on your garments, then you will find the Kingdom of Heaven.**

6 **Whatever you shall bind on earth shall be bound in Heaven; and whatever you shall loose on earth shall be loosed in Heaven. If two of you shall agree on earth as touching anything that they shall ask, it shall be given to them by the power of the Spirit.**

7   For where the Children of God are gathered together with faith and belief in the Truth, the Spirit is in the midst of them."

CHAPTER 21
ON SAVING LIVES

1   When the time had come, Jesus made plans to journey to Jerusalem for the Feast of the Tabernacles. So he sent messengers before him and they went, entering a village of the Samaritans, to make ready for them, for it was a long journey.

2   Since the messengers were preparing for the Jewish Feast in Jerusalem, the Samaritans rejected them; for the Samaritans believe that they alone worship the true religion of Israel at Mount Gerizim, not in Jerusalem. So the messengers returned and reported to Jesus.

3   When his disciples James and John, the sons of Zebedee, heard of this rejection, they asked, "Master, is it your will that we command fire from Heaven to consume them?"

4   Jesus rebuked them, saying **"You know not what manner of Spirit we are. The Son of Man has not come to bring suffering to men's lives, but to save them from suffering."**

5   So the messengers were sent to another village to prepare for the journey.

CHAPTER 22
THE FEAST OF THE TABERNACLES

1   Now the Feast of Tabernacles was close at hand. His disciples therefore said to him, "Depart now and go into Judea so others may hear the doctrine of Love and Truth."

2   Jesus said to them, **"My time has not yet come, but your time is ready, for they do not seek to silence you. You go to**

the Feast now. I plan to go to the Feast later." Therefore he stayed a while in Galilee after his disciples had departed. Later he began the journey to the Feast.

3   Some sought him at the Feast and said, "Where is he?" And there was much murmuring amongst the people concerning him. Some said, "He is a good man;" others said, "No, he stirs the people."

4   Now in the midst of the Feast Jesus arrived and went up into the temple to teach. The people were astonished, saying, "How does this man know these things, having never been taught?"

5   Jesus answered, **"The Truth is not mine, but His that sent me. If any man will do His will, he shall know Truth, whether it be of God, or whether I speak of it myself. He that speaks of himself seeks his own fame; but he that seeks His fame that sent him, speaks Truth. Do not judge according to appearance, judge instead in Spirit."**

6   Certain of the Pharisees heard what Jesus said and that the people murmured great things concerning him; they feared the doctrine he taught. So the chief priests sent officers to take him if he spoke a blasphemy.

7   On the last day of the Feast, Jesus continued his teachings, saying, **"Yet a little while I am with you, and then I go to Him that sent me. If any man thirsts, let him come to me and drink. He that drinks the Living Water knows Truth."**

8   Many of the people, when they heard the teachings of Jesus, said, "Truly this is a Prophet, for he speaks as one having authority of the Spirit and not as the scribes." Hearing Jesus speak, the officers left him untouched.

9   When the officers returned to the chief priests they asked, "Why have you not brought him?"

10 The officers answered, "No one has ever spoken like this man."

11 The chief priests then asked, "Are you also deceived? Have any of the rulers or any of the Pharisees believed him?"

12 But Nicodemus said to them, "Does our law judge any man before it hears him and knows the Truth?"

13 They answered, "Are you also of Galilee? Search and look; for out of Galilee arises no prophet."

CHAPTER 23
THE WOMAN ACCUSED OF MANY SINS

1 Jesus then went to the Mount of Olives. Early in the morning he came again to the temple. Many people came to him; so he sat down and taught them.

2 Some Pharisees and scribes brought to him a woman accused of many sins. When they had set her in their midst, they said to him, "Master, this woman was found in adultery, in the very act. Moses in the law commanded that such should be stoned. But what do you say?"

3 They said this, tempting him, that they might have something with which to accuse him.

4 Jesus wrote on the ground with his finger, as though he had not heard them. So when they continued asking him, he said to them, **"He that has not sinned amongst you, let him throw the first stone."**

5 And no one dared to do so; for having examined themselves and being convicted by their own conscience, they departed one by one.

6 When Jesus stood up and saw none of the accusers, he asked her, **"Where are your accusers? Has no one condemned you?"**

7 She said, "No one."

8 Jesus answered, **"Neither do I condemn you.**

9 **I bring the Light of the world. He that follows Truth shall not walk in darkness, but shall have the Light of the world. They judge after the flesh; I judge in Spirit.**

10 **Truly, I say to you, if you continue with the Light, then you are my disciple indeed. You shall know Truth and the Truth shall set you free."**

CHAPTER 24
THE PARABLE OF THE GOOD SAMARITAN

1 Journeying around Judea, Jesus was teaching when a lawyer stood up and asked, "Master, we have been taught, An eye for an eye and a tooth for a tooth; but I have heard you say, Love your enemy as your neighbor. Who then is my neighbor?"

2 Jesus answered, **"A man went from Jerusalem to Jericho, a very dangerous road, and fell amongst thieves. They stripped him of his clothing and wounded him, then departed, leaving him half dead.**

3 **By chance a Priest of the Kohanim came that way; when he saw him, he passed by on the other side. And likewise a Levite, when he was at the place, came and looked on him, and passed by on the other side.**

4 **But a certain Samaritan, as he journeyed, came where he was. When he saw him suffering he had compassion on him; went to him; bound up his wounds, pouring on oil and wine; set him on his own beast; brought him to an inn; and took care of him.**

5   The next day when he departed, he took out two pence and gave them to the innkeeper, saying, Take care of him; whatever more you spend, when I come again, I will repay you.

6   Now, which of these three do you think was a neighbor to him that fell amongst the thieves?"

7   The lawyer said, "He that showed mercy on him."

8   Jesus said to him, **"Go and do likewise; this is the law and the prophets."**

CHAPTER 25
ON THE HYPOCRISY OF AUTHORITIES: NEGLECT OF LOVE AND TRUTH

1   After Jesus spoke, some Pharisees and others sought to dine with him. So he went with them and sat down to eat. Certain of the Pharisees found fault that he had not washed before dinner.

2   Jesus said to them, **"You make clean the outside of the cup and the platter; but within, you are insatiable and corrupt. You fools, did not He that made that which is outside make that which is within also?**

3   **You give donations of such things as you have and, behold, all things are clean to you.**

4   **Woe unto you! For you tithe mint, rue and other herbs, but neglect Love and Truth; these you should have done, but not neglect the other.**

5   **Woe unto you! For you love the uppermost seats in the synagogues and greetings in the markets.**

6   **Woe unto you, hypocrites! For you are as graves that are not seen; the men that walk over them are not aware of them."**

DENIAL OF KEY OF KNOWLEDGE

7   Then one of the lawyers said to him, "Master, thus saying you rebuke us also."

8   Jesus replied, **"Woe unto you also! For you laid men with burdens difficult to be borne and you yourselves touch not the burdens with one of your fingers.**

9   **Woe unto you! For you build monuments to the prophets and your fathers killed them.**

10 **Truly you bear witness that you approve the deeds of your fathers; for they indeed killed them and you build their monuments.**

11 **Therefore said the wisdom of God: I will send them prophets and apostles. Some they shall kill and some they shall persecute: that the blood of all the prophets, which was shed from the beginning, from the blood of Abel to the blood of Zacharias, may be required for Truth.**

12 **Woe unto you! For you have taken away the Key of Knowledge, the Holy Soma, from those that seek to enter the Kingdom of Heaven. You do not enter yourselves and those that seek to enter you hinder by persecution and arrest."**

13 After he said these things, certain of the Pharisees became enraged and began to vehemently urge him to speak; lying in wait for him, seeking more out of his mouth, that they might have something with which to accuse him.

CHAPTER 26
ON BEING A SON OF GOD

1   Returning to Jerusalem for the Feast of the Dedication, Jesus walked into the temple.

2   The people came around him, and said to him, "How long will you make us doubt? If are the Son of God, tell us plainly."

3   Jesus answered, **"I testified and you do not believe.**

4   **You believe not; because you are not the Living Father's Children. His Children have been anointed with the Holy Soma. They know Truth and hear my voice. They have seen Heaven's Glory in the Clear Light and they shall have Eternal Life.**

5   **The Children of God and the Heavenly Father are one. The Living Father in Heaven is greater than all; and no man is able to pluck them out of His hand.**

6   **The teachings and works that I do in the Living Father's name, they bear witness of me, a Son of God."**

7   Then the people took up stones to stone him.

8   Jesus asked, **"Many good works I have shown you from the Living Father; for which of those works do you stone me?"**

9   The people answered him, saying, "For good works we do not stone you; but for blasphemy; because you, being a man, make yourself a God."

10   Jesus answered, **"Truly, I say to you, is it not written in the scripture, *You are Gods*? It has been so since the Holy Fruit, the Key of Knowledge, was first eaten. If he called them Gods, unto whom the Word of God came, and the law cannot be broken; how can you say, You blaspheme, of him whom the Living Father has sent into the world, anointed, and now says, I am a Son of God?**

11   **If I do not the works of the Living Father, believe me not. But if I do, though you do not believe me, believe the works: that you may know, and believe, that the Heavenly Father is in me, and I in Him, as with all the Children of God."**

12 The people then laid down their stones, for he spoke as one having authority of the Spirit and not as the scribes.

13 Hearing of this, the chief priests, elders, and scribes sought how they might put him to death; as they feared his doctrine, calling it blasphemy.

CHAPTER 27
THE PARABLE OF THE LOST SON

1 Jesus went teaching through the towns and villages journeying from Jerusalem. Jesus told this parable:

2 "A certain man had two sons; the younger of them said to his father, Father, give me the portion of goods that fall to me. So he divided unto them his fortune.

3 Not many days after the younger son gathered his belongings together, journeying to a far country. There he wasted his substance with riotous living. When he had spent all, there arose a mighty famine in that land; and he began to be in want. He went and joined himself to a citizen of that country, who sent him into his fields to feed swine. He would have willingly filled his belly with the husks that the swine ate, but no man gave to him.

4 Then he thought to himself, How many of my father's hired servants have Bread enough to spare, while I perish with hunger! I will arise and go to my father. I will say to him, Father, I have sinned against Heaven and before you. I am no longer worthy to be called your son; make me as one of your hired servants.

5 So he arose and went to his father. But as he approached, his father saw him and had compassion. Running to him he hugged and kissed him.

6   The son said to him, Father, I have sinned against Heaven and in your sight; I am no longer worthy to be called your son.

7   But the father said to his servants, Bring forth the best robe and put it on him. Put a ring on his hand and shoes on his feet. Bring forth a fatted calf and kill it. Let us eat and celebrate. For my son was dead and is now reborn; he was lost and is now found. So they began to celebrate.

8   Now his elder son was in the field. As he came close to the house, he heard music and dancing. He called one of the servants and asked why they were celebrating. The servant said to him, Your brother has come home and your father has killed a fatted calf, because he has received him safe and sound.

9   The elder son was angry and would not go in. Therefore his father came out and pleaded with him. He answering said to his father, Look, these many years I served you and never transgressed at any time your commandments. Yet, you never gave me a fatted calf that I might celebrate with my friends. Instead, as soon as this son comes home, devoured by riotous living, you have killed a fatted calf for him.

10   The father said to him, Son, you are always with me and all that I have is yours.

11   We should celebrate and be glad. For your brother was dead and is now reborn; was lost and is now found."

CHAPTER 28
THE PARABLE OF
THE WORKERS IN THE VINEYARD

1   When Jesus had finished this teaching, he departed and went to the coast of Judea. Jesus teaching told them another parable:

2   "The Kingdom of Heaven is like a man that is a landowner who went out early in the morning to hire laborers for his vineyard; when he had agreed with the laborers for a penny a day, he sent them into his vineyard.

3   He went out about the third hour and saw others standing idle in the marketplace. So he said to them, You also go into the vineyard and whatever is right I will give you. And they went their way.

4   Again he went out about the sixth and ninth hour; and did likewise.

5   About the eleventh hour he went out and found others standing idle. He said to them, Why do you stand here idle all day?

6   They said to him, Because no man has hired us. He said to them, You also go into the vineyard and whatever is right, that you shall receive.

7   So when evening came, the Lord of the vineyard said to his steward, Call the laborers and pay them their hire, beginning from the last unto the first.

8   When they came that were hired last, every man received a penny. So when the first hired came, they expected that they should receive more, but every man likewise received a penny.

9   When they had received it, they murmured against the Good landowner, saying, These last have worked but one hour; you have made them equal to us that have borne the burden and heat of the day.

10 But he answered them, saying, Friend, I do you no wrong. Did you not agree with me for a penny? Take that which is yours and go your way. I will give to the last as to you.

11 **Is it not lawful for me to do what I will with my own? Is your eye evil because I am Good? So the last shall be first and the first shall be last. Many called, but few chosen."**

CHAPTER 29
OUTSIDE OF JERUSALEM:
ON THE PASSION

1 As the Passover was near, they began traveling to Jerusalem. While resting on their way, Jesus began telling them more of the things that would happen to him, **"We will go to Jerusalem. The Son of Man shall suffer many things. He will be delivered unto chief priests, elders, and scribes. They shall condemn him to death and shall deliver him to the Gentiles. They will mock him, whip him, spit upon him, and crucify him. The Son of Man will suffer much for the Love of God and man."**

2 They were amazed and afraid. A certain young disciple then asked, "Master, we know you will depart from us. Who then is to be our leader?"

3 Jesus said to them, **"Wherever you are, you are to go to my brother James."**

4 Then Jesus took Judas aside and spoke with him privately.

5 When he returned, the other disciples asked Judas, "What did the Master say to you?"

6 Judas did not tell them, saying "If I told you what he asked of me, you would be consumed by fire from Heaven and stone me."

SUPPER WITH LAZARUS

7 Later that day, Jesus and the disciples arrived in Bethany, just outside of Jerusalem, where they were made supper.

8   Lazarus, who had been as the lost son, was one of them that sat at the table with them. They were exceedingly glad and celebrated.

9   Mary took a pound of very costly spikenard ointment and anointed the feet of Jesus, wiping his feet with her hair. The house was filled with the odor of the ointment.

10   Then Simon Peter asked, "Why was this ointment not sold for three hundred pence and given to the poor?"

11   Jesus answered, **"Let her alone. She has done what she could for the poor. For the day of my burying she has kept this ointment. The poor will be with you always, but me you will not have always. Truly, I say to you, wherever the Truth is taught throughout the world, what she has humbly done for Love shall be remembered."**

12   Many people knew that Jesus was there and came to see him, for he taught as one having authority of the Spirit and not as the scribes. They came not only to see Jesus, but also to see Lazarus, who had been born again, as had been many others that Jesus taught.

13   The chief priests consulted that they might also silence Lazarus; because by reason of his testimony many believed in the teachings of Jesus and became disciples.

CHAPTER 30
JESUS IN JERUSALEM:
TRIUMPHANT ENTRY

1   Jesus sent forth two of his disciples, James and Simon, when they came close to Jerusalem, around the Mount of Olives. He told them, **"Go into the village of Bethphage and as soon as you enter you shall find a donkey and her colt tied. Free them and bring them to me. When a man says to you, Why do you do**

this? You reply, The Master has need of them. He will then send them here."

2 The two disciples went their way and found the donkey and her colt tied by a door outside a place where two ways met. They freed them. A man that stood there said to them, "Why do you do this, freeing the donkey and colt?"

3 They said to him as Jesus had directed and he let them go. So they brought the donkey and colt to Jesus and cast their garments on them.

4 Jesus sat upon the colt as he entered Jerusalem. Many spread their garments on the way. Others cut down branches off the trees and strewed them on the way.

5 They that went before and they that followed cried, saying, "Hosanna; Blessed is he that comes in the name of the Lord: Blessed be the kingdom of our father David, that comes in the name of the Lord: Hosanna in the highest. Blessed be the Son of David. Blessed be the King of Israel. Blessed be the Messiah."

6 Jesus arrived at the temple and went inside to pray.

7 After Jesus had prayed and the evening had come, he went back to Bethany with the disciples.

CLEANING OF THE TEMPLE

8 The next morning, when journeying to Jerusalem, around Bethphage, Jesus was hungry. Seeing a fig tree that he had known for many years as having leaves, but no fruit, he again went to it so he might find a fig thereon. When he came to it, he again found nothing but leaves; it did not bear Good Fruit.

9 Jesus said to it, **"Many chances have been given to you to bear Good Fruit. Now therefore, no one will eat fruit of you hereafter."**

10 Arriving at the temple, Jesus went inside. He began to cast out those that bought and sold in the temple, overthrowing the tables of the moneychangers and the seats of those that sold doves. He would not suffer that anyone should carry any merchandise through the temple.

11 He taught, saying to them, **"Is it not written, *My house shall be called a house of prayer for all nations*? But you have made it a den of thieves. The Temple must be clean for the Kingdom of Heaven."**

12 When evening came, Jesus and the disciples left Jerusalem.

13 The chief priests and elders, hearing of how Jesus entered into Jerusalem, the multitude that followed him, and his cleaning of the temple, became even more determined to silence him.

ON THE POWER OF FAITH AND BELIEF

14 In the morning as they returned to Jerusalem, they passed by the same fig tree on the way by Bethphage. They saw it had dried up from the roots and was ready to be cut down.

15 Simon Peter recalling what Jesus had said the previous day, said, "Master, behold, the fig tree which you curst has withered away."

16 Jesus answered, **"Begin with faith as little as a grain of Mustard Seed. Truly, I say to you, the Children of God, whoever shall say to this mountain, Be removed and cast into the sea, or say to the sea, Calm thy water while I walk on thee; with no doubt in his heart, but believes that those things which he said shall come to pass, he shall have whatever he said.**

17 **Therefore I say to you, What things you seek, when you pray, believe that you shall receive them; and you shall have them provided by the power of the Spirit in Heaven."**

CHAPTER 31
TEACHINGS OF THE TEMPLE:
THE PARABLE OF THE COVETOUS TENANTS

1   When Jesus arrived at the temple, chief priests, elders, and scribes came to him. Jesus then spoke to them a parable.

2   "A powerful man planted a vineyard and set a hedge about it. He dug a place for the wine and built a tower, renting it out to tenants. He then departed into a far country.

3   At the season he sent to the tenants a servant so he would receive payment from the tenants. Instead, they caught him, beat him, and sent him away empty handed.

4   Again he sent to them another servant. At him they cast stones, wounded him in the head, and sent him away shamefully handled.

5   Again he sent another and they killed him. He sent many others; some were beaten and some were killed.

6   Having a son, his beloved, he sent him to them last, saying, They will reverence my son.

7   But the tenants said amongst themselves, This is the heir. Let us kill him and the inheritance shall be ours. So they took him and killed him, casting him out of the vineyard.

8   What shall therefore the Lord of the vineyard do?

9   He will remove the tenants and rent the vineyard to others. Have you not read this scripture: *The stone which the builders rejected has now become the corner stone; this is the Lord's doing and it is marvelous in our eyes?*"

10   The chief priests and elders wanted to arrest him then because they knew that he had spoken the parable against them; but they

feared they might stir the people to revolt if they did so by day. So they left to plot his arrest.

ON THE SEPARATION OF SPIRITUAL AND MATERIAL WORLDS

11 Now certain of the Pharisees sought to catch him in his words. They said to him, "Master, we know that you are true, for you regard not appearances, but teach the way of the Lord. Is it lawful to give tribute to Caesar or not? Shall we give or shall we not give?"

12 Jesus, knowing their hypocrisy, said to them, **"Why do you test me? Bring me a penny, that I may see it."**

13 They brought it to Jesus.

14 He asked, **"Whose is this image and inscription?"**

15 They said to him, "Caesar's."

16 Jesus answered, **"Render unto Caesar the things that are Caesar's, and to God the things that are God's."**

17 They were astonished at his saying.

ON LIFE AFTER DEATH

18 Then certain Sadducees, who believe there is no Life after death, came to him. They asked him, "Master, Moses instructed us, If a man's brother dies and leaves his wife behind him, and leaves no children, his brother should take his wife and have children. Now there were seven brethren. The first took a wife and dying left no children. The second took her and died, leaving no children. The third was likewise. The seven had her and left no children. Last of all, the woman died also. After death, when they are reborn, whose wife shall she be? For the seven had her as wife."

19 Jesus answered, **"You err, because you know neither the scriptures nor the power of God. When they are born again, they neither marry nor are given in marriage; but are as Angels in Heaven. Truly, I say to you, our Heavenly Father is not the God of the dead, but the God of the Living. You therefore do err greatly."**

ON LOVE

20 One of the scribes, having heard them reasoning together, perceiving that he had answered them well, asked him, "Which is the greatest commandment of all?"

21 Jesus answered, **"To Love.**

22 **You have heard the commandment:** *The Lord our God is One, and you shall love the Lord thy God with all your heart, with all your Soul, and with all your strength.*

23 **And the commandment: Love your neighbor as yourself.**

24 **Truly, I say to you, there are no other commandments greater than the commandments to Love."**

25 The scribe said to him, "Well, Master you have said the Truth. For there is one God and there is none other but He. And to love Him with all your heart, with all your Soul, and with all your strength, and to love your neighbor as yourself, is more than all the burnt offerings and sacrifices."

26 When Jesus saw that he answered discreetly, he said to him, **"You are not far from the Kingdom of Heaven."**

27 After that, no one dared ask him a question, for he taught them as one having authority of the Spirit and not as the scribes.

CHAPTER 32
ON THE FUTURE

1   As they left the temple, Simon Peter said to him, "Master, Jerusalem has many magnificent buildings well-built of stone!"

2   Jesus said, **"Behold this Temple and these great buildings! The day will come when they will be destroyed; there shall not be one stone left upon another: be careful not to stumble upon them, or become a stone that others stumble upon."**

3   Jesus and the disciples then came to the Mount of Olives where they would rest the remaining nights they had together. As they sat, Simon Peter asked him, "When shall these things of which you speak happen? What shall be the sign when these things shall be fulfilled?"

4   Jesus answered, **"The Truth must first be published in all nations for all peoples; but the day or hour no one knows; neither myself nor the Angels in Heaven. Only our Heavenly Father knows all these things.**

5   **Beware lest any man deceive you; by their Fruits you shall know them.**

6   **When you hear of wars and rumors of wars, be not troubled, for such things need be. Nation shall rise against nation and kingdom against kingdom. There shall be earthquakes, floods, and famines.**

7   **Be mindful you keepers of Truth. You will be delivered up to councils; you will be beaten; and you shall be brought before rulers and kings for the Sacred Mysteries, for a testimony against them.**

8   **But when they deliver you up, be not anxious for tomorrow, neither premeditate: before you speak about these**

things. Whatever shall be provided to you in the moment, speak that; for it is not you that speaks, but the Holy Spirit.

9   Now brother shall betray brother; the father the son; children shall rise up against their parents; and cause them to be put in prison or to death, all for the Truth and Sacred Mysteries.

10 You shall be hated for Truth's sake. He that finds the Kingdom of Heaven shall endure to the last."

CHAPTER 33
ON THE SACRED MYSTERIES

1   Jesus then said to his disciples, **"Many teachings have been given to you. It is to you, the worthy, that the Sacred Mysteries of the Kingdom of Heaven have first been revealed. You have been anointed with the Flesh and Blood of our Living Father in Heaven; as I am anointed. Truly, I say to you, the Age will come, and will be known, when the Sacred Mysteries shall be revealed to all peoples.**

2   **Whoever finds the interpretation of my teachings will be as Christ, reborn to Eternal Life. Seek until you find. When you find you will be astonished, as thunder in a perfect mind.**

3   **The Kingdom of God is all things: the first and the last; the Holy and the profane; the bride and the bridegroom; the honored and the scorned; the ruler and the slave; the strong and the weak; the young and the old; the wise and the senseless; the sound and the silence; the Infinite and the finite; control and the uncontrollable; Love and hate; knowledge and ignorance; war and peace; wealth and poverty; union and dissolution; judgment and acquittal; Life and death. His Kingdom is all these things and more.**

4   **All things come from God through the Holy Spirit. Split a piece of wood, and there He is. Lift up a stone and you will**

find Him. All natures, all formations, all creatures exist in and with one another. The Holy Spirit is the primary force of all Creation; like the wind, you cannot see it, yet it touches all things."

5 Jesus continued with his teachings, saying **"You have been shown how to prepare the Holy Soma, the Flesh and Blood of our Living Father. He covers the naked and heals the sick. The blind man sees and the lame man walks. Let those who seek, find what they seek: the Key of Knowledge; let them receive the Treasure. Let them find what was lost: the Truth.**

6 **When you have been anointed with the Holy Soma, you will see with the Clear Light and be born again with a pure Soul, finding Eternal Life in the Holy One. Weakness and diseases will have gone. Illuminated with the Divine Light, the forces of darkness will have fled in terror."**

7 Jesus then said, "Remember my teachings. Many shall come in my name and shall deceive many. If those that lead you say, See, the Kingdom of Heaven is in the air, then the birds of the air will precede you. If they say to you, It is in the sea, then the fish of the sea will precede you. Rather, the Kingdom of Heaven is within you. When you come to know and understand this Truth you will be first in the Kingdom, as the Children of God."

CHAPTER 34
THE LAST SUPPER

1 In preparation for the Passover, his disciples said to him, "Master, where should we go and prepare to eat supper?"

2 He sent forth two of his disciples, James and Simon, telling them, **"Go into the city. There you shall meet a man bearing a pitcher of water; follow him. Where he goes in, say to the good man of the house, Master said, Where is the guest chamber where I shall eat with my disciples? He will show**

you a large upper room furnished and ready. There make preparations for us."

3 His disciples went forth and came into the city. They found as he had said to them and they made preparations.

4 In the evening, Jesus came with the disciples. Upon arrival, Jesus laid his garments aside. He took a towel and wrapped it around himself; preparing, he poured water into a basin. He then began to wash the feet of the disciples, wiping them with the towel.

5 When he came to Simon Peter, he asked Jesus, "Master, why do you wash our feet?"

6 Jesus answered, **"What I do now you shall understand later."**

7 Simon Peter said to him, "Master, do not wash my feet like a servant."

8 Jesus answered, **"If I do not wash you, you will have no part with me."**

9 Simon Peter then said to him, "Then Master, wash not only my feet, but my whole body."

10 Jesus answered, **"He that is washed in Truth is clean all over, and your Temple is clean; but I must now wash your feet."**

11 After Jesus had washed their feet, he sat down and asked them, **"Do you know the meaning of what I have done for you?**

12 **You call me Master. Truly, I say to you, the servant is not greater than his master; neither is he that is sent greater than the Heavenly Father that sent him.**

13 **If I then, your Master, have humbled myself washing your feet; you also ought to wash others' feet. For I have given you an example, that you should do as I have done for you. If you understand these things, happy are you if you do them.**

14 **So this is my teaching: Humble yourself for Love; as I have Loved you, you must Love one another.**

15 After this, they prepared to eat supper. As they ate, he told them, **"Tonight we will perform the Sacred Ceremony. It will forever be a covenant between the Holy One and those that seek Truth."**

16 Jesus blessed and broke the anointed Bread, giving it to them, saying, **"Take, eat; this is the Living Father's Flesh, the Sacramental Soma, that is given for those that seek to be reborn to Eternal Life."**

17 He took a cup of wine and when he had given thanks, he said to them, **"Drink, this is the Sacramental Blood, the Truth, which is shed for many."** He gave the cup to them. They all drank of it.

18 Jesus then said, **"Truly I say to you, I will drink no more of the Fruit of the Vine until that day that I drink it in the Kingdom of Heaven."**

19 His brother James responded saying, "And I will not eat the Living Bread from this hour until I see you born again as Christ."

20 As they sat and ate, Jesus said, **"One of you which eat with me shall lead to my death."**

21 Then the disciples looked at one another, doubting of whom he spoke. Now there was leaning on Jesus' bosom his beloved disciple. Simon Peter therefore beckoned to Mary to ask who it was of whom he spoke. Lying on Jesus' breast the beloved disciple asked him, "Master, who is it?"

22 Jesus answered Mary discreetly, **"He it is to whom I shall give a piece of Bread, when I have dipped it."** When he had dipped the Bread, he gave it to Judas. Then Jesus said to him, **"What you must do, do quickly."**

23 No man at the table knew for what intent he spoke this to him. For some of them thought, because Judas had a bag, that Jesus had said to him, Buy those things that we have need of; or, that he should give something to the poor. Judas, having received the Bread, went immediately out into the night as Jesus instructed.

24 Judas then went to meet with the chief priests to arrange the arrest of Jesus later that night, away from the multitudes, so as to not stir a revolt with his followers.

25 After supper, Jesus said, **"I know whom I have chosen that the scripture may be fulfilled. He will be cursed for generations, yet he has sacrificed the most.**

26 **Now I tell you this before it comes; so that when it comes to pass, you may believe. Truly, I say to you, he that receives whomever I send receives me and he that receives me receives Him that sent me."**

27 Jesus then had them form a circle; holding hands, they sang a hymn. After, they departed for the Mount of Olives to rest for the night.

CHAPTER 35
THE ARREST OF JESUS

1 On the way, Jesus told them, **"All of you shall forsake me this night; for it is written,** *Strike the shepherd and the sheep will be scattered.***"**

2 But Simon Peter said to him, "I will not forsake you."

3   Jesus said, **"Truly, I say to you, this very night you shall deny me."**

4   But Simon Peter spoke more vehemently, "If I should die with you, I will not deny you in any way." Likewise they all said.

5   When they came to a garden called Gethsemane at the Mount of Olives, he said to his disciples, **"Rest here while I pray."**

6   He then took Simon Peter and the sons of Zebedee a stone's throw away from the others. Jesus began to be deeply troubled and anguished. He said to them, **"My Soul is overwhelmed with sorrow waiting for death; stay here: watch and pray."**

7   He went forward a little and fell to the ground, his Spirit being tested; praying that if it was possible, the hour might pass from him. He said, **"Father, all things are possible to you; please take this cup from me; nevertheless, not what I will, but what you will."**

8   Jesus turned and found them sleeping. He said to them, **"You sleep? Could you not watch one hour? Watch and pray, lest you find yourself tested. The Spirit is truly ready, but the flesh is weak."** Again he went and prayed, speaking the same words.

9   When he turned, he found them sleeping again.

10   He came a third time and said to them, **"Rest, you have had enough. The hour has come. Behold, the Son of Man is to be lead to his crucifixion. Rise up, let us go; the time is at hand."**

11   Immediately, while he spoke, Judas came with a band of men and officers of the chief priests with swords and staffs. He had given them a sign, saying, "Whomever I shall kiss, that same is Jesus; take him and lead him away safely."

12 As soon as he came, he went to Jesus, saying, "Master, master," and kissed him. So the band of men laid their hands on him.

13 Simon Peter then drew a sword.

14 Jesus restrained him saying, **"Put away the sword, for those who live by the sword shall die by the sword. Would you have us not Drink from the Cup that God has given us?"**

15 The band of men and officers bound Jesus and took him away.

16 His disciples then forsook him and fled; but one followed closely behind Jesus, a certain young man, Simon, having a linen cloth wrapped about his body. An officer approached the young man to take him, but he cast his linen cloth to the ground; thereon he trampled the garment and fled from them naked.

17 Jesus then said, **"Behold, a Son of God."**

CHAPTER 36
AT THE PALACE:
JESUS BEFORE THE HIGH PRIEST

1 The band of men and officers took Jesus to the palace of the high priest hours before the sunrise. There he faced the judgment of the high priest and his assembled Sanhedrin council: chief priests, elders and scribes.

2 Simon Peter followed Jesus from afar to the palace. He sat with the servants and warmed himself at the fire.

3 The high priest sought testimony against Jesus to put him to death. Chief priests, elders and scribes bore witness of many things against him, but they did not agree amongst themselves.

4 The high priest stood up in the midst and asked Jesus, "Answer you nothing? What is it that these witnesses say against

you? Have you not violated the Sabbath? Have you not stirred the people with Soma? Do you not claim to be the King of Israel, the Messiah?"

5   But he held his peace and answered nothing.

6   Then the high priest asked him, "You have tasted Soma and now you claim to be the Son of God?"

7   Jesus answered, **"Yes and you shall see Christ sitting in the clouds of Heaven."**

8   The high priest then tore his clothes in disgust, saying, "What need do we have of any further witnesses? You have heard the blasphemy. What do you think?"

9   They then found him guilty and condemned that he should be put to death. Some then began to strike him and spit on him.

PETER'S DENIAL OF JESUS

10 As Simon Peter was beneath in the palace, there came one of the maids of the high priest. When she saw Simon Peter warming himself, she looked upon him and said, "You were with Jesus of Nazareth."

11 But Simon Peter denied this, saying, "I know not, neither do I understand what you say." He then went out into the porch.

12 Another maid saw him and said to them that stood by, "This is one of them."

13 Simon Peter denied it again.

14 After a little while, they that stood by said to Simon Peter, "Surely you are one of them. Your speech is that of a Galilean."

15 Simon Peter began to curse and to swear, saying, "I do not know this man of whom you speak."

16 Later Simon Peter called to mind the words that Jesus said to him, "You shall deny me." When he thought thereon, he wept.

CHAPTER 37
JESUS BEFORE PILATE AND HEROD ANTIPAS

1 Early that morning the high priest had Jesus bound and carried away, delivering him to Pilate for final judgment; for under Caesar's law they could not put any man to death.

2 Pilate asked him, "Are you the King of the Jews?"

3 Jesus answered, **"Say you this thing of yourself, or did others tell it to you?"**

4 Pilate answered, "Am I a Jew? Your own high priest has delivered you to me to be put to death. What have you done?"

5 Jesus answered, **"My Kingdom is not of this world. If my Kingdom were of this world, then my servants would fight so I would not be delivered to death."**

6 Pilate therefore asked him, "You are a king then?"

7 Jesus answered, **"You say that I am a king. To this end I was born and for this cause I came into the world: that I should testify to the Truth of the Kingdom of Heaven in all its Glory. Every one that knows Truth hears my voice."**

8 Pilate said to him, "What is truth?"

9 After he had said this, he went out to the chief priests that brought Jesus and said, "I find no fault in him."

10 They were then even fiercer, saying, "He stirs the people openly with Soma and his teachings throughout the land; beginning from Nazareth to Jerusalem."

11 When Pilate heard of Nazareth, he asked whether Jesus was of Nazareth in Galilee. As soon as he found that he belonged to Herod's jurisdiction of Galilee, he sent him to Herod Antipas, who was in Jerusalem at the time.

12 Herod questioned him in many words, but Jesus said nothing to him. The chief priests stood, vehemently accusing him of stirring the people against them. But Herod, fearful that he would further arouse the people against him as he had by beheading John the Baptist, returned him to Pilate without judgment.

13 Pilate, when he had called the chief priests, said to them, "You have brought this man to me, as one that perverts the people. But, neither I nor Herod, having examined him found any fault in this man touching those things of which you accuse him."

14 Since it was the custom at Passover to release one prisoner, Pilate offered to the multitude gathered in the courtyard to release Jesus, or another man called Barabbas, who was imprisoned for stirring sedition. Unknown to Pilate, the chief priests, elders, and scribes had made certain that their people were in the courtyard.

15 The multitude therefore cried out saying, "Crucify Jesus; release Barabbas."

16 Pilate then had no choice but to release Barabbas. But, still willing to release Jesus, Pilate said to the chief priests, "I will whip Jesus and release him also."

17 The chief priests answered him, "By the law he ought to die because he made himself King and Son of God."

18 Concerned with Caesar's law, Pilate went again into the judgment hall and asked Jesus, "Who are you? Are you a King? Are you a Son of God?" Jesus gave him no answer. Then Pilate

asked him, "Do you not know that I have the power to release you and the power to crucify you?"

19 Jesus answered, **"You have no power at all against the Kingdom of Heaven."**

20 When Pilate heard this he was offended. He then decided to deliver Jesus for crucifixion, but not before having Jesus stripped of his clothing and whipped. The soldiers made a crown of thorns, putting it on his head, and they put a purple robe on him, saying, "Hail, King of the Jews!"

21 Jesus returned wearing the crown of thorns and the purple robe. Pilate then said to the chief priests, "Behold, the King of the Jews!" Pilate wrote a title to be put on the cross: *Jesus of Nazareth, King of the Jews.*

22 The chief priests said to Pilate, "Write nothing; for he is not our King."

23 Pilate answered, "What I have written I have written."

CHAPTER 38
THE CRUCIFIXION

1 After they had mocked him, they took off the purple robe and put his own clothes back on him, leading him out to crucify him. They compelled a certain young man who had heard the Truth taught by Jesus to bear his cross.

2 They brought Jesus to a place called Golgotha, which means the place of the skull, where they crucified him. Two others were crucified with him: two thieves; one on his right and the other on his left.

3 After they had crucified Jesus, the soldiers took his garments and made four parts, to every soldier a part. But the coat of Jesus was without seam, woven from the top throughout. Therefore, the

soldiers said, "Let us not cut it, but cast lots for it to see whose it shall be," which they did. Thus the scripture was fulfilled that said, *They divide my garments amongst them and for my coat they cast lots.*

4   The title, *Jesus of Nazareth, King of the Jews*, was read by many people, for the place where Jesus was crucified was close to the city. Some that passed by railed on him, shaking their heads saying, "Save yourself and come down from the cross."

5   Likewise, the chief priests mocking said amongst themselves and with the scribes, "He saved others; but he cannot save himself. Let the Son of God descend from the cross so we may see and believe."

6   Now there stood by the cross of Jesus his mother; his mother's sister, Mary the wife of Cleopas; and Mary Magdalene.

7   When Jesus saw his mother and Mary Magdalene standing by, he said to his mother, **"Woman, behold thy son!"** Then he said to his beloved, **"Behold thy mother!"** And from that hour forth they were as Mother and Child, sharing the same home.

8   Jesus then cried with a loud voice, saying, **"My God, my Holy Soma, why have you forsaken me?"**

9   After this, Jesus said, **"I thirst."**

10   One ran and filled a sponge full of the Fruit of the Vine, put it on a reed, and gave Drink to Jesus, saying, "Let us see whether God will come to take him now."

11   A while after Jesus had received Drink, he said, **"Heavenly Father, into your hands I commend my Spirit. It is finished,"** bowing his head and giving up the Spirit.

12   Because bodies should not remain upon the cross on the Sabbath day, the chief priests asked Pilate that their legs be broken so that they would die swiftly and their bodies could be

taken away before sunset. The soldiers, therefore, broke the legs of the two that were crucified with Jesus.

13 But when they came to Jesus and saw that he was dead already, they did not break his legs. Instead, one of the soldiers with a spear pierced his side. Immediately there came out blood and water. Thus the scripture was fulfilled that said, *They shall look on him whom they pierced.*

CHAPTER 39
THE BURIAL

1 Before the evening had come, Joseph of Arimathea, a Councilor of the Sanhedrin and disciple, went boldly to Pilate, asking for the body of Jesus.

2 Pilate marveled that he was already dead. He called the centurion, asking whether Jesus was indeed dead. When he confirmed it with the centurion, he consented to the release of the body.

3 Joseph and Nicodemus, who had not agreed with the Sanhedrin judgment, then took the body of Jesus along with some other disciples.

4 Near Golgotha there was a garden in which Joseph had a new sepulcher that had been cut out of rock. There they prepared the body of Jesus for burial, rolling a stone before the entrance to be the door of the sepulcher.

CHAPTER 40
BORN AGAIN AS CHRIST:
AT THE SEPULCHER

1 When the Sabbath was past, Mary Magdalene early, while it was still dark, came to the sepulcher, and saw that the stone had been taken away from the sepulcher and the body of Jesus was gone. Then she ran to Simon Peter and a certain other disciple,

saying to them, "They have taken our Master out of the sepulcher and I know not where they have borne him."

2   The three therefore went forth and came to the sepulcher. The beloved disciple, stooping down and looking in, saw burial linen clothes lying there, but did not go in.

3   Simon Peter then went into the sepulcher, finding no body and seeing the linen clothes. Then the other disciple entered the sepulcher and saw the same. Not knowing what had happened to the body of Jesus, they departed and went to their own homes, except for Mary.

4   Mary stood without at the sepulcher weeping. As she wept, a voice asked her, **"Woman, why do you weep?"**

5   She turned and saw a man standing there, not knowing who it was. The man asked her again, **"Woman, why do you weep? Whom do you seek?"**

6   She, supposing him to be the gardener, said to him, "Sir, if you have borne him from here, tell me where he is and I will take him away."

7   The man then said to her, **"Mary."**

8   She said to him, "Master," for she then knew Christ was in him.

9   The man then told her, **"Go to my brethren, and say to them, the Son of Man ascends unto my Father and your Father; and to my God and your God."**

10   Mary departed, telling the disciples that she had seen Christ and that he had spoken these things to her.

THE ROAD TO BETHEL

11 Shortly after this, Cleopas, a disciple of Jesus, and Simon, were on the road to a place called Bethel. They talked together of all these things that had happened. It came to pass that while they communed and reasoned together, a man drew near and went with them.

12 He asked them, **"What manner of communications are these that you have? Are you sad?"**

13 One of them answered, "Are you a stranger in Jerusalem? Do you not know the things that came to pass therein these days?"

14 He asked them, **"What things?"**

15 They answered, "Concerning Jesus of Nazareth, who was a prophet mighty in deed and word before God and all the people. The chief priests, elders, and scribes delivered him to the Gentiles to be condemned to death and he was crucified."

16 A certain women of our company made us astonished, when she arrived early at his sepulcher and found his body was gone. Others came and found no body. Now we are told she saw him born again as Christ.

17 Then he said to them, **"Fools; you are slow of heart to believe all that the prophets have spoken."** Beginning at Moses and all the prophets, he expounded to them the scriptures of the things concerning Christ.

18 As they drew close to Bethel, the man made as though he would go on. But they constrained him, saying "Eat with us." So he joined them.

19 As he sat at meal with them, he broke the bread and anointed it in accordance with the Sacred Ceremony. Giving the Bread to

them, their eyes were then opened. They knew him as Christ. He then departed.

20 They then said one to the other "Did not our heart burn within us while he talked and opened to us the scriptures?"

IN JERUSALEM

21 The following day they returned to Jerusalem. Finding the disciples and others gathered together, the two told them they had seen Christ, he having performed the Sacred Ceremony with them. That same evening where the disciples were assembled, a man appeared and stood in their midst saying to them, **"Peace be unto you."**

22 Then the disciples were glad, as they recognized Christ in him.

23 The man said to them again, **"Peace be unto you. As my Father has sent me, even so Christ sends you."** When he had said this, he broke the bread and anointed it in accordance with the Sacred Ceremony. Giving them the Bread he said to them, **"Receive the Holy Spirit."**

24 James hesitated, for he had sworn that he would not eat the Living Bread from that hour wherein he had drunk the cup of Sacramental Wine with Jesus until he saw him born again as Christ. Seeing this the man said, **"My brother, eat your Bread, for the Son of Man has been born again as Christ."**

AT THE SEA OF GALILEE

25 Days after, some of the disciples were at the Sea of Galilee: James the Righteous; James and John, the sons of Zebedee; Simon Peter; Simon; and two others.

26 In the evening, Simon Peter said to them, "I am going fishing." Some of the other disciples went with him. They went forth in a boat, but they caught nothing.

27 When the morning had come, a man stood on the shore. The man asked them, **"Have you any meat?"**

28 They answered him, "No."

29 He told them, **"Cast the net on the right side of the boat and you shall find."**

30 They cast the net as told but were not able to draw it in for the multitude of fish caught. Thereon Mary Magdalene, who was on shore, said, "It is Christ." Now when Simon Peter heard the voice of Mary, he cast himself into the sea, for he was naked.

31 The other disciples came in a little boat to help retrieve the net full of fish. When they had come close to land, they saw bread and a fire of coals for the fish to be laid thereon.

32 The man told them, **"Bring the fish which you have caught."**

33 Having dressed, Simon Peter drew to land the net with the multitude of fish. There were so many, yet the net was not broken. After they had prepared the fish and laid them on the coals, the man said to them, **"Come and dine."**

34 None of the disciples dared to ask, "Who are you?" They knew that Christ was in him.

35 The man then broke bread and fish, performing the Sacred Ceremony, saying to the disciples **"Follow Christ in Love and Truth."**

36 After they had dined, he said to the disciples, **"Go forth and Feed the people."**

37 Then Simon Peter, turning about, saw the beloved disciple. Simon Peter, believing females were unworthy, asked, "What shall this disciple do?"

38 He said to him, **"Our Father decides who is worthy. If the Holy One wills this disciple wait, what is that to you? You go forth and follow Christ."**

THE ASCENSION

39 Some 40 days after Jesus was born again as Christ, the disciples gathered at the Mount of Olives, communing with the Sacramental Soma. In a Heavenly Vision, Jesus appeared to them as Christ.

40 Simon Peter asked him, "Will the Kingdom of God be restored at this time?"

41 He answered, **"Remember my teachings. What you look forward to has already come. The Kingdom will not come by waiting for it. It is not a matter of saying, Here it is, or There it is. For behold, the Kingdom of God is all Creation. But many do not see it.**

42 **The Holy Spirit has come upon you to open your eyes. You shall be witnesses to the Truth to the far parts of the earth."**

43 After he had spoken these things the disciples were illuminated with the Divine Light; their clothing glowed with a luminous, white Light. Then there appeared two others in Angelic Glory. Suddenly they disappeared into the clouds of Heaven. A voice then said, "As Christ is in Heaven, he shall return in like manner." Amen.

ANALYSIS

Preliminary Comments

An objective review of *The Gospel of Simon* clearly discloses that most of the text closely parallels *The New Testament* gospels.[31] Although not empirically calculated, it is estimated that at least 80 per cent of the text is consistent with *The New Testament*. Contrary wise, various parts deviate from *The New Testament* gospels, consistent with other sources, such as known Gnostic texts. This analysis will concentrate on the significant differences and differing interpretations that can be drawn from the text when compared to *The New Testament* gospels.

The most significant differences between *The Gospel of Simon* and the accepted *New Testament* gospels center in six areas:

1. The Sacramental use of an Entheogenic Substance: the Holy Soma;
2. Divinity for All the Children of God;
3. Equality of Women
   (e.g. Mary Magdalene, Beloved Disciple);
4. The Rehabilitation/Elevation of Simon Peter;
5. The Role of Judas; and
6. Jesus, the Savior – Sin vs. Suffering

During the life time of Jesus, any one of the first three would be considered blasphemy and a challenge to the existing order. Even to this day, the use of entheogenic substances and divinity for all the Children of God (i.e., anyone can become a Child of God like Jesus) are outside generally accepted Christianity. While the equality of women has significantly improved in the Western world since biblical times, their religious equality is still sometimes lacking (e.g., priesthood in the Roman Catholic Church).

Before examining these six areas and other items of interest in detail, a discussion of the evolution of early Christianity is in order.

Evolution of Early Christianity

The New Testament gospels are generally agreed by scholars to have been written between AD 65 and AD 100 by later associates of the apostles,[32] with *Mark*[33] the earliest, followed by *Matthew*,[34] *Luke*,[35] and *John*.[36] Over 30 years elapsed from the crucifixion of Jesus to the earliest known written gospel. Consequently, the gospels themselves relied upon an oral tradition dependent upon memory and repetition or a Q source (e.g., written sayings, similar to *The Gospel of Thomas*).[37] Such sources readily permitted revision of subject matter as stories were retold.

Once committed to writing, the now accepted gospels were not produced and preserved by printing press and computer memory, but rather by hand written copying. While copying provides a somewhat reliable medium, it also permits variation for the purposes of literary refinement, as well as revision due to political and religious pressures.

It is the political and religious pressures of the early centuries of Christianity that are of particular interest as it relates to *The Gospel of Simon*, as well as non-canonical texts of the period, especially *The Gospel of Thomas*.[38]

The early Christian church consisted of widely disparate sects, geographically and philosophically. Communication over thousands of miles was difficult at best. As a result, variances in beliefs and practices developed.[39]

Additionally, a philosophical gulf developed between what ultimately became the accepted Roman Catholic Church and what may be generally referred to as the Gnostic sects; although the Gnostic sects themselves varied widely in specific beliefs and practices.[40] For the purpose of this analysis, the Gnostic belief being proposed and analyzed refers to that most similar to a characteristic of Theosophy: the innate ability to directly commune with God.[41]

To generalize, the developing Catholic Church followed the traditional Judaist model with a priesthood that limited direct access to God (with the inclusion of Jesus, the only son of God), while the Gnostic model of *The Gospel of Simon* followed a more revolutionary approach that recognized the individual's ability to directly access God personally (via Gnosis) as taught by Jesus. Ironically, the earliest Christian communities may have been more Gnostic in nature, outnumbering those communities that were considered heretical and ultimately developed into the Roman Catholic Church.[42]

The Gnostic sects in particular presented a serious challenge to authority, whether it was the developing Catholic Church or Roman Empire, since it permitted direct access to God without an intermediary.[43] A private, unique experience of God is essentially spiritually anarchistic, requiring no authority structure. This is not meant to mean that Gnostic sects had absolutely no authority structure, but rather they were less amenable to such, likely accounting for the wider variation between the various Gnostic sects. *Simon* 8:14 (and *John* 4:21-24) suggest a more Gnostic approach, without authority structure.

The battle between these two extremes raged for over 300 years. Finally, the Catholic Church centered in Rome, backed by the power of the Roman Empire, prevailed, resulting in a consolidation of accepted texts and destruction of non-canonical texts.[44] It is important to note that the political interests of the Roman Empire were better served by supporting the Catholic Church, since it had a hierarchal structure that would support control of its subjects, whereas the revolutionary Gnostic sects presented far more difficult problems when it came to controlling the individual.[45]

With this developmental background in mind, an analysis of the most significant areas of interest is presented.

The Sacramental use of Entheogenic Substance: the Holy Soma

The use of entheogenic substances by ancient cultures was widespread and is undisputed by historians.[46][47][48] Sometimes the entheogenic substances were available to the community at large as a sacrament and sometimes they were kept a closely guarded secret, for use by the shaman, medicine man or similar priestly person.[49][50]

As various societies and religions became more structured and powerful, many of the ceremonies and sacraments were prohibited or became ritualized substitutions for the original methods, typically in response to persecution by authorities. In his milestone book *Ceremonial Chemistry*, Thomas Szasz documents that throughout history, users of drugs, including entheogens, have been persecuted and marginalized by authorities, whether religious, political or medical.[51]

Is Christianity one of those religions that used entheogenic substances in its early, formative days? Did early Christians hide their entheogenic practices in order to avoid persecution? Were these entheogenic practices hidden in coded language so that only those who were privy to the secret knowledge would understand its spiritual meaning? Most of today's scholars would answer an unequivocal "no."

One of the first scholarly efforts postulating early Christianity's use of entheogenic substances was *The Sacred Mushroom and the Cross*.[52] In this landmark work, John M. Allegro proposed that early Christianity grew from a fertility based cult that used the entheogenic mushroom (Amanita muscaria) as a sacrament. He maintained that when such practices had to be written down, they would use coded language in the stories being told to keep them secret in order to avoid persecution.[53]

Allegro's philological analysis is so complex that it is beyond the understanding of all but the most knowledgeable scholars in the given subject area. It is likely that for this reason alone it received severe criticism at the time of publication. While there is more scholarly support for this thesis today than when the book was first published in 1970, it is still far from generally accepted.[54] [55] Consistent with Allegro's hypothesis, *The Gospel of Simon* essentially decodes the secrets hidden in *The New Testament* gospels, identifying the entheogenic substance as the Holy Soma.

Rather than the psychedelic mushroom proposed by Allego, another entheogenic substance to be considered is Mandrake, a psychedelic plant belonging to the nightshade family, also thought to have fertility or aphrodisiac qualities by some.

Allegro posited that Mandrake of *The Old Testament*[56] was really the Mushroom.[57] Whether Mushroom or other entheogenic substance, *The Old Testament* contains two interesting references to Mandrake.

The first is in *Genesis* 30:14-17, involving two wives of Jacob: Rachel offers to provide her night with their husband in exchange for Leah providing Mandrakes that had been harvested from the fields. Certainly Mandrakes would have to be of significant value to provide consideration for such an exchange.

A more interesting reference may be found in the *Song of Solomon* 7:13:

> The mandrakes give a smell,
> and at our gates *are* all manner of pleasant
> *fruits*, new and old,
> *which* I have laid up for thee, O my beloved.

Simon 12:12-15 contains comparable references of related significance (also found in *Matthew* 13:44 and 13:52), with Jesus saying:

> "...The Kingdom of Heaven is like a Treasure hid in a field; which when a man has found, he hides, and for joy thereof goes and sells all that he has and buys that field...."

...Therefore every scribe that is instructed in the Kingdom of Heaven is like a man that is a house owner, who brings forth out of his laid up Treasure, things new and old."

The reference in Solomon to pleasant *fruits* (i.e., Treasure) at the gates (i.e., of Heaven) is consistent with many *New Testament* parables. That these are preceded by the smell of Mandrakes, along with the reference to Treasure "new and old," makes for an intriguing parallel.

Who but a scribe would be well versed in the *Song of Solomon*? A scribe would have had access to instructional use of the Mandrake (Mushroom or other entheogen) as a key to the Kingdom of Heaven.

An additional curiosity regarding the Mandrake is that it is sometimes disparagingly referred to as "Satan's Apple."[58] The apple reference is to the Garden of Eden story (*Genesis* 2:8-20 and 3:1-24) wherein Eve and Adam eat of the Tree of Knowledge. God tells Adam that if he were to eat of the tree, he shall "surely die."

Eve is talked into eating the fruit by a cunning serpent that tells her that "...your eyes shall be opened and you shall be as gods...." Having eaten the fruit, Eve and Adam become aware of their nakedness and become ashamed. The consequence of their actions is to be cast from the Garden of Eden (*Genesis* 3:22-23), with God saying "...Behold, the man is become as one of us, to know...." This Garden of Eden episode is most likely what Jesus was referring to when calling himself a Son of God in *Simon* 26:10 (see parallel in *John* 10:33-36).

Whether the Mandrake was the fruit eaten in the Garden of Eden is conjecture. However, it is not the only entheogenic reference to the Garden of Eden. A fresco in the 12th century Plaincourault Abbey in Indre, France, depicts the Tree of Knowledge as mushrooms. Various authoritative sources have speculated that the fresco represents the entheogenic Amanita muscaria mushroom.[59][60]

Another possible entheogenic source is ergot, from which the powerful psychedelic lysergic acid diethylamide (LSD) may be prepared using the process of hydrolysis. Ergot is a fungus that grows on grains, notably barley. In Greece, barley was used to prepare Kykeon, a drink used in the Eleusinian Mysteries; it is quite possible that ancient peoples discovered a method of preparing an LSD like substance from the ergot fungus obtained from barley.

This possibility is documented in detail in *The Road to Eleusis*, co-authored by R. Gordon Wasson (ethno-mycologist and author, particularly in the area of ancient civilizations use of entheogens), Albert Hoffman (chemist; discoverer of LSD), and Carl A. P. Ruck (professor of classical studies, notably ancient Greece).[61]

Alexander the Great's conquests of the third century BC extended Greek culture throughout the Middle East, including Israel and Egypt.[62] Consequently, knowledge of the Eleusinian Mysteries extended beyond ancient Greece.

The Eleusinian Mysteries revolved around the myth of the goddess of agriculture, Demeter, and the related themes of death, rebirth, and eternal life. The rites and ceremonies performed were kept secret, but from what is known, initiates would have visions and believed that they would be rewarded in the afterlife as a result of participation in the mysteries.[63]

Interestingly, Kykeon is prepared using water and barley. Of particular relevance in this respect is *The Homeric Hymn to Demeter*[64] where the goddess Demeter refuses to drink red wine, but accepts Kykeon instead.[65] This certainly evokes the miracle performed by Jesus where he turned water into a "good" wine or drink (*John* 2:1-12 and *Simon* 8:1-6).

Another point of interest is the Jewish tradition before the 12th century AD that Passover would begin in the first month (Nisan), determined by when the barley crop was ripe.[66] Barley provides an extremely effective medium for growing ergot, especially when ripe.

Not only was barley directly related to the determined start of Passover, but it was also the bread of choice for Jesus when feeding the 5,000. *John* 6:1-13 (see related *Simon* 15:1-13) identifies the feeding of the 5,000 with barley bread around the time of the Passover. Feeding 5,000 people with a small quantity of barley bread would be a difficult problem indeed.

The solution to the mystery resides in the tremendous potency of LSD like substances. A dose of LSD suitable to induce a spiritual state in one person is about 150 micrograms;[67] 5,000 doses would be 750,000 micrograms, the equivalent of less than three hundredths of an ounce. *Simon* 15:1-12 describes how the barley bread, anointed with an entheogenic substance, was used to feed the 5,000 so they were "filled" with the Kingdom of Heaven; the task could easily be accomplished with a powerful entheogenic substance like LSD (additionally, LSD often is an appetite suppressant).[68]

The Gospel of Simon clearly supports the hypothesis of early Christianity's use of entheogenic substances. Although the specific substances used are not identified, the use of natural substances, referred to as Holy Soma, to induce spiritual states and visions is weaved throughout *The Gospel of Simon*. Specific areas of entheogenic interest follow.

The Visit of the Magi (*Simon* 5:1-7)

Among the first to pay their respect to the newborn Jesus was the Magi, as recorded in *Matthew* 2:1-14. The meaning of the term magi has evolved over the millennia to a somewhat pejorative term relating to magic or magician. Certainly *Matthew* did not intend to imply that meaning to the visit.

The original reference is generally agreed to relate to the followers of Zoroaster (i.e., wise men), which provides much more insight into the visit.[69] Zoroaster was a prophet dating to anywhere between 1700 BC and 500 BC, depending upon the source relied upon. In their religion, they used a sacred plant referred to as Haoma, which was said to have many spiritual benefits, including that of conferring immortality. Interestingly, the Sanskrit word for Haoma is Soma.[70]

Soma

The Rig Veda,[71] one of the four sacred texts of Hinduism, dating to around 1700 BC to 1100 BC,[72] prominently mentions Soma. *Rig Veda* 9.74.1-9 (Mandala number/Hymn number/Stanza numbers) describes the preparation of Soma for the "great feast," in a manner similar to the Zoroastrians.[73]

R. Gordon Wasson, the famous ethno mycologist, hypothesized in 1968 that Soma was the psychedelic Amanita muscaria mushroom.[74] Allegro suggested the same.[75]

In *The Road to Eleusis* Documentation chapter, Carl A. P. Ruck, citing linguist Calvin Watkins, notes the corresponding similarity in preparation of the Eleusinian Mysteries *Kykeon* and Vedic *Soma*; thereby hypothesizing Ergot as the entheogenic source.[76,77]

Others believe it was Cannabis,[78] Ephedra,[79] or some other entheogenic plant substance.[80] In any event, the various descriptions of Soma in *The Rig Veda* indicate it is a powerful, sacred plant of psychedelic effect.

Consider this excerpt from *Rig Veda* 8.79.2-6 regarding the power of Soma:

> ...He covers the naked and heals all who are sick. The blind man sees; the lame man steps forth....Let those who seek find what they seek: let them receive the treasure....Let him find what was lost before; let him push forward the man of truth....

Reading these words, one cannot help but notice the similarity with words from the Sermon on the Mount (*Simon* 11:37 and *Matthew* 7:7-8). Of even greater significance is the implication of the blind seeing and the lame walking. Are the gospels describing literal miracles or the figurative effects of entheogenic plants as described in *The Rig Veda*?

Numerous references may be found in *The Rig Veda* to the "light," "heaven," and "immortality." *Rig Veda* 8.48.3 states:

> ... We have drunk the Soma; we have become immortal; we have gone to the light ....

The ninth Mandala of *The Rig Veda* is entirely devoted to Soma, with these significant references:[81]

> The Sage of Heaven ... sends us delightful powers of Life .... He the bright Son .... magnified the Single Eye .... drive away dark shades .... Make the paths ready .... Make the lights shine .... win the light. (Hymn 9);

> ... they are purified ... in the waters they are rinsed .... cleansed .... pure ... the Soma ... slayer of sins.... (Hymn 24);

> .... The Sun and all his forms of light .... This Soma being purified...Slayer of sins....(Hymn 28);

> .... They decorate the Child of Heaven .... From every side, O Soma ... filled full of riches .... (Hymn 33);

> ... make the lights shine brightly .... May Soma pour all treasure of the Heavens ... Upon the liberal worshipper .... to the height of Heaven .... (Hymn 36);

> The Child, when blended with the streams, speeding the plan of sacrifice .... (Hymn 102);
>
> .... The Mighty One was born Immortal, giving Life, lighting darkness with His shine .... (Hymn 108); and
>
> ... place me in that deathless, undecaying world wherein the Light of Heaven is set .... Make me immortal in that realm where dwells the King, Vivasvan's Son, where ... the secret shrine of Heaven, where ... those waters .... Flow .... (Hymn 113).

The words of *The Rig Veda*, describing the effects of Soma, parallel many of the descriptions of heaven, light, rebirth, and eternal life found in the gospels. *Simon* clearly incorporates this vision in various parts.

Interestingly, the Greek word "Soma" translates to the English word "body."[82] *The New Testament* covenant of eating the body (Soma) of Christ (e.g., *Matthew* 26:26) in communion demonstrates the secret coded language referred to by Allegro and revealed by *The Gospel of Simon*.

The Clear Light and Rebirth

The Bardo Thodol, otherwise known as *The Tibetan Book of the Dead*, frequently references the Light and the Clear Light in its description of death and rebirth.[83] Likewise, both *The Old Testament* and *The New Testament* contain numerous references to God and Light.

As previously discussed, the Garden of Eden's Tree of Knowledge has been hypothesized to represent an entheogenic source. God tells Adam that he will surely die if he eats of this tree; when he does, God himself says in *Genesis* 3:22 "...Behold, the man is become as one of us, to know...." Thus, God casts them from the garden "...lest he put forth his hand, and take also of the Tree of Life, and eat, and live forever...."

The gospels in general and *John* 3:3 in particular, emphasize the need to be reborn to achieve eternal life. *The Gospel of Simon* conceptually integrates these references to Light, death, Life, and rebirth (see *Simon* 9:1-9).

Of particular interest in this respect is the book published in 1964 by Timothy Leary, Ralph Metzner, and Richard Alpert: *The Psychedelic Experience: A Manual Based on the Tibetan Book of the Dead*.[84] The authors came to the insightful conclusion that the psychedelic experience; ingestion of entheogenic mushrooms, peyote, or ergot (i.e., LSD) for example; had a parallel to death and rebirth. Accordingly, they adapted *The Tibetan Book of the Dead* to assist the users of entheogenic substances during their experience to achieve spiritual enlightenment and rebirth.

Death is a necessary precedent to rebirth. God tells Adam that he will surely die if he eats the forbidden fruit, but left unsaid is the path to rebirth, although God places heavenly beings and a flaming sword to protect the Tree of Life (*Genesis* 3:24). Jesus reveals the path back to Eden – to the Kingdom of Heaven – the path to rebirth and eternal life.

In summary, the entheogenic substance referred to as the Holy Soma in *The Gospel of Simon* cannot be definitely identified. However, the substance would have to be powerful enough to evoke a communion with God, including components such as a death/rebirth experience, a sense of immortality, and an awesome perception of Creation as seen with the Light of God. Likely candidates would be ergot, mushrooms, peyote, and cannabis. It is quite possible that no one substance was the Holy Soma; rather, differing substances may have been used based on circumstance and availability.

Divinity for All the Children of God

As discussed in the analysis comments "Evolution of Early Christianity," a battle raged in the early church between the developing Catholic position that Jesus was the one and only Son (i.e., Child) of God, and the revolutionary position that Jesus revealed the way for anyone to become a Child of God – a Gnostic approach. *The Gospel of Simon* is clearly Gnostic, with some similarities to *The Gospel of Thomas*.

The Gospel of Simon is consistent with this Gnostic interpretation as can be clearly seen in *Simon* 12:19 (On the Kingdom of Heaven: Within Your Temple) and *Simon* 33 (On the Sacred Mysteries) and alluded to in other chapters. Common passages between *The Gospel of Simon* and *The Gospel of Thomas* can be found at various points.

Much of *The New Testament* gospels could be interpreted within the Gnostic paradigm (e.g., *Luke* 17:21). However, over time the Catholic interpretation prevailed, primarily due to *The Gospel according to John*. Elaine Pagels concludes in *Beyond Belief: The Secret Gospel of Thomas* that the influential, second century Bishop Irenaeus, known for his attack on Gnostics, was uniquely responsible for the subsequent interpretation of the gospels by the Roman Catholic Church, in a manner contrary to Gnosticism.[85]

Further, Pagels maintains that *John* was most likely written as a refutation of the gnostic *Gospel of Thomas*. Pagels' conclusions are amply supported by the evidence cited, although it is possible that the original "*John*" was Gnostic in character and was subsequently modified, not only to refute *Thomas*, but to support the Catholic interpretation of the nature of Jesus.

The revision of *John* over time is easily demonstrated by the evidence.[86] The famous story of the "Woman taken in Adultery" (*John* 7:53-8:11) was clearly added to *John* at a later date.[87] The earliest known texts of John do not include such a story. The story first appears in texts of the fourth century (around the time that texts considered heretical were being destroyed), whereas it is believed that *John* was originally written around AD 90-100.[88]

Interestingly, a story of "A Woman Accused of Many Sins" is referenced by Eusebius (citing Papias, circa AD 100) as appearing in the lost (or destroyed) *Gospel of the Hebrews*.[89] This particular gospel is cited by Eusebius as one of the disputed books (along with other books that were subsequently included in *The New Testament*), as opposed to a rejected book, which may account for addition of this story to *John* at a later date.[90]

The addition of this story is no small matter. While it may be a true story of the ministry of Jesus, the blatant addition of this story at a much later date is a testimony to the possible revisions made by others over time. If a significant revision such as this can be made, then much smaller revisions over time could easily be justified.

In this regard, *The Gospel according to John* as we know it may have been a rewrite of an earlier Gnostic work by Cerinthus (a contemporary and alleged opponent of John). According to Gaius of Rome, a respected Christian writer of the early third century, the books attributed to John (the *Gospel* and *Revelation*) were in fact written by Cerinthus.[91] [92] While the evidence is murky at best, it would provide an explanation for the evolution of *The Gospel according to John* and its residual Gnostic elements.

The revisions of interest to the Catholic vs. Gnostic battle over the nature of divinity relate to *The Gospel according to John* vs. *The Gospel of Thomas*. As previously stated, Pagels maintains that *John* was written as a refutation of *Thomas*.

While *The Gospel of Thomas* found at Nag Hammadi likely dates to around AD 200, it is believed by some that the original work dates to as early as AD 40.[93] The document has many of the same sayings as found in *The New Testament* gospels, but written from a Gnostic perspective around the time, or possibly before, the accepted synoptic gospels were first written. *Thomas* could very well be a "Q" source for the synoptic gospels (*Matthew* and *Luke* in particular).

Thomas does not recount any scenes from the resurrection of Jesus. In fact, the gospel dwells on the Kingdom of Heaven and the Kingdom of God existing on earth at that time. *Thomas* 3 and 113 indicates this, stating "... the Kingdom is inside you, and it is outside you...." and "... the Kingdom of the Father is spread out upon the earth, but people do not see it."

Consequently, the gnostic *Gospel of Thomas* would not only be at odds with the Catholic interpretation of the nature of Jesus, but also at odds with the resurrection portions of the other gospels (or not in direct support of such). Thus a gospel was needed to refute *Thomas*.

As noted by Pagels, the synoptic gospels only mention Thomas as one of the disciples. There are no other mentions of the disciple Thomas or stories referencing him. Notably, *The Gospel of Thomas* starts off stating that it is being written by Didymus Judas Thomas. Only in *The Gospel according to John* is Thomas referred to as Didymus. *John* continues with three pertinent references to Thomas (Didymus), all of which are disparaging.

First, when Jesus discusses raising Lazarus from the dead (*John* 11:11-15), Thomas is said to express a lack of understanding or faith in the divine actions of Jesus (*John* 11:16).

Second, when Jesus discusses his death and alludes to his resurrection (*John* 14:1-4), Thomas again expresses a lack of understanding (*John* 14:5).

Third and foremost, are the appearances of Jesus to the disciples after his crucifixion (*John* 20:11-21:23). In only two of the appearances is he clearly recognized as Jesus; in the others, he is seen as a man that the disciples believe is Jesus.

In the instances where Jesus is recognizable (*John* 20:19-29), he appears to the disciples showing his wounds. Thomas is absent when he first appears and confers the Holy Spirit on the apostles (implying that Thomas is no longer an honored apostle). When Thomas arrives late, he says he will only believe if he can inspect the wounds. Consequently, the next appearance to the disciples enables Thomas to inspect the wounds and recognize the resurrected Jesus. *John* gives the final rebuke to the "Doubting Thomas," with Jesus saying "blessed are they that have not seen, and yet have believed."

There is no reason for *John* to specifically identify Thomas as Didymus other than to clearly reference the reader to *The Gospel of Thomas* and proclaim its heresy regarding the nature of divinity and the resurrection.

But *The Gospel according to John* went even further in its revisionism. *John* was written (or rewritten) to diminish the role of women, particularly Mary Magdalene, and rehabilitate, at least partially, the role of Simon Peter.

Equality of Women (e.g. Mary Magdalene, Beloved Disciple)

A feature of distinction in *The Gospel of Thomas* is the role of women, specifically Mary Magdalene. Traditional Judeo-Christian religious groups of the time were plainly male dominated, yet women played a prominent role in the ministry of Jesus.

Mary's presence and participation is clear in *Thomas,* as well as many other non-canonical texts of early Christianity. At the end of *Thomas* (114), Simon Peter says to Jesus:

> "Make Mary leave us, for females are not worthy of Life."

Jesus responds saying:

"Look, I shall guide her ...." to "... the
Kingdom of Heaven."[94]

The developing Catholic Church could not have their leader, Simon Peter, condemning women in such a manner. While the early church was not ready to embrace an equal role for women, it recognized that women played an important role in the ministry of Jesus. Accordingly, *John* toned down the anti-women rhetoric attributed to Simon Peter.

Both *Thomas* and *John* end in a somewhat similar manner, with a discussion between Jesus and Simon Peter. In *Thomas* there is the previously quoted dialogue between Jesus and Simon Peter regarding Mary's fate, while in *John* 21:20-22 there is Simon Peter asking Jesus about the beloved disciple's fate; Jesus responds to Simon Peter to the effect that if Jesus wants the beloved disciple to:

"... tarry till I come, what is that to thee?
Follow thou me."

This certainly represents a rebuke to Simon Peter. *Simon* 40:37-38 provides the following.

37 Then Simon Peter, turning about, saw the beloved disciple. Simon Peter, believing females were unworthy, asked, "What shall this disciple do?"

38 He said to him, "Our Father decides who is worthy. If the Holy One wills this disciple wait, what is that to you? You go forth and follow Christ."

It is certainly a curiosity as to why the beloved disciple would not go forth to spread the gospel with the other disciples: unless of course that disciple was a woman.

Tradition has it that the author or source of *John* was the beloved disciple, possibly John. None of the other accepted gospels even mention the beloved disciple. Contrary wise, *The Gospel of*

Simon explicitly identifies the beloved disciple as Mary Magdalene.

The evidence for Mary Magdalene as the beloved disciple is admittedly circumstantial. As previously discussed, the early church needed to refute the words attributed to Simon Peter in *The Gospel of Thomas* regarding women without elevating Mary Magdalene to a disciple status that would be on par with the original, twelve disciples.

Consequently, *John* obfuscated the discussion between Jesus and Simon Peter to conceal the identity of Mary Magdalene while not refuting her place outright. An outright repudiation of Mary Magdalene was not possible in the early days of Christianity as her role was all too well known and numerous texts identified her as much loved by Jesus (e.g., *The Gospel of Philip* and *The Gospel of Mary*).[95]

Another rationale for Mary Magdalene as the beloved disciple may be found by a reading of *John* 13:21-30 (related to *Simon* 34:20-24). Here we have Simon Peter asking the beloved disciple, who is leaning on the bosom of Jesus, to ask Jesus who will betray him. In a private discussion between Jesus and the beloved disciple, Jesus tells the beloved disciple it is the one to whom he gives the sop of bread, Judas. Jesus then proceeds to tell Judas to do what he has to do and *John* 13:28 states "Now no man at the table knew for what intent he spake this unto him."

Given the scene described by *John*, the beloved disciple was right there, asking the question to which Jesus responded. The beloved disciple was in a position to hear and see all that took place, to in fact know the intent of the words spoken. But as admitted in *John*, "no man" knew the intent; but a woman did.

An additional rationale for Mary Magdalene as the beloved disciple may be found by a reading of *John* 19:25-26 (related to *Simon* 38:6-7). In *John* 19:25, the persons standing by the cross are specifically listed (including his mother and Mary Magdalene), with no identification of any male disciples. In the following paragraph, *John* 19:26, Jesus is said to have seen his mother and the beloved disciple standing by, then stating "Woman, behold thy son!" This statement has typically been interpreted as referring to the beloved disciple, but could just as easily refer to Jesus himself.

Finally, there is the appearance of Jesus to the disciples at the Sea of Galilee. In *John* 21:1-14 (see related *Simon* 40:25-38), a man appears to the disciples telling them to cast their net to the right side of the boat. When they do so, they catch a "multitude of fishes." At this point the beloved disciple identifies the unrecognizable Jesus as "the Lord," upon which Simon Peter jumps into the water.

When the fish were brought ashore, the total fish caught were identified as 153. Since the gospel had already stated that a multitude of fish had been caught, why was it necessary to provide a specific number? Who would take the time and trouble to count all the fish? What is the significance of 153?

The answer lies in Greek isopsephy, the practice of adding up the number values of each letter in a word to calculate a single number. This practice is most commonly known relative to the number 666 (or alternately 616),[96] the Number of the Beast, which is contained in *The Revelation of Jesus Christ to John*.[97]

Both *The Revelation of Jesus Christ to John* and *The Gospel according to John* use isopsephy. Applying isopsephy in Greek to the name "Mary Magdalene" results in the number 153.[98] An editor of *John* purposely inserted the number 153 to be certain that the knowledgeable reader would know that the beloved disciple was Mary Magdalene, despite the obfuscation.

That the beloved disciple is Mary Magdalene better explains the reason for Simon Peter jumping into the water when he was naked (*John* 21:7 and *Simon* 40:30). Simon Peter was not concerned with being seen naked by the male disciples; and he certainly had been seen naked by Jesus before as they had been traveling the countryside together for years. The reason he jumped into the water upon hearing the beloved disciple's voice was that he did not want to be seen naked by a woman – Mary Magdalene.

Critics of Mary Magdalene as the beloved disciple can point to the parts of *John* that use the masculine pronoun to identify the beloved disciple. The explanation for this also resides at the end of *The Gospel of Thomas* (114). When Simon Peter states to Jesus that females are not worthy of Life, Jesus responds saying "... I shall guide her to make her male...."

Consequently, *John* 21:22 makes her male, stating "If I will that he tarry till I come, what is that to thee?" Thus the beloved disciple waits for Jesus to lead her/him to the Kingdom of Heaven.

Interestingly, Mary Magdalene is the only person cited by the canonical gospels as having witnessed the three major final events in the ministry of Jesus: the crucifixion, the burial, and the discovery of the empty tomb. Also, she (i.e., the beloved disciple) consistently identifies Christ or the Lord in an otherwise unrecognizable man after the discovery that the body of Jesus was missing from the tomb.

The fact that Mary Magdalene and other women were critical to the ministry of Jesus is clearly stated in *Simon* 10:9, while more generally acknowledged in other gospels (e.g., *Luke* 8:1-3). The diminished role for women after the crucifixion of Jesus can best be explained by the rehabilitation and elevation of the role of Simon Peter, who was not favorably inclined towards woman per both *Thomas* and *Simon*.

The Rehabilitation/Elevation of Simon Peter

In the early days of Christianity, Simon Peter's image was in serious need of rehabilitation. Not only did *Thomas* and *Simon* have Simon Peter believing that women were unworthy of Life, but the gospels demonstrated that he had a significant lack of faith and understanding in the teachings of Jesus. Noteworthy instances include:

Mark 8:32-33 and *Matthew* 16:22-23. Simon Peter objects to the crucifixion fate of Jesus, wherein Jesus rebukes Simon Peter, saying "Get behind me, Satan," and elaborating that he is concerned with the things of men, not God. *Simon* 19:8-9 has similar quotes.

John 13:8. Simon Peter objects to Jesus washing his feet: a lesson in Love for one another. *Simon* 34:7-8 has similar quotes.

John 18:10-11. Simon Peter draws a sword to defend Jesus from being arrested; he is restrained in his violent effort by Jesus (*Mark* 14:47, *Matthew* 26:51-52 and *Luke* 22:50-51 recount the episode without specific reference to Simon Peter). *Simon* 35:13-14 has similar quotes.

Mark 14:69-70, *Matthew* 26:73-75, *Luke* 22:54-62, and *John* 18:15-27. All four gospels agree, in a rarity, that Simon Peter denied knowledge of Jesus when questioned. *Simon* 36:10-16 has similar quotes.

As previously discussed, *The Gospel according to John* was written or rewritten not only to rebut *The Gospel of Thomas*, but to obfuscate Mary Magdalene's role in the ministry of Jesus as well as hide Simon Peter's beliefs about the worthiness of women. These changes alone went a long way to enabling the future role of Simon Peter. However, more revisions were necessary.

The gospels are commonly read to include a mandate from Jesus that Simon Peter head the Christian church as it went forward. The lynch pin for this interpretation is found in *Matthew* 16:18, in which Simon Peter is identified as the rock upon which the church will be built. This is the sole gospel that provides such a mandate.

Conflicting with this supposed mandate, *Thomas* 12 identifies James, in the words of Jesus, as the first leader of the church after the death of Jesus (consistent with *Simon* 29:2-3). Clement of Alexandria, sometime around AD 190, confirmed this when he said that Jesus had selected James as his successor (as recorded by the church historian Eusebius).[99] James was in fact the leader of the church in Jerusalem after the death of Jesus.

Contrary to *Thomas*, *Simon*, and other evidence (Clement and Eusebius), *Matthew* 16:16-18 has Jesus appointing Simon Peter as his successor. This particular part of *Matthew* is most likely a revision made later in time; another response to *The Gospel of Thomas*.

The key to understanding this revision is the use of the name "Simon Peter." Both *Thomas* and *John* primarily use the name Simon Peter (further support for the linkage of *John* being a refutation of *Thomas*).

The synoptic gospels rarely use the name Simon Peter: *Mark* does not use that name at any time; *Matthew* uses it once; and *Luke* uses it once; other than when Jesus provides the surname Peter to Simon.

The one time use of the name Simon Peter by *Matthew* is particularly interesting, as it is in the story where Simon Peter recognizes Jesus as the Son of God and Jesus appoints Simon Peter as head of the church (*Matthew* 16:16-18).

Clearly the author (revisionist) seeks to directly tie this part of *Matthew* to *Thomas*, in a direct refutation. This was necessary because *Thomas* 13 has Simon Peter saying that Jesus is merely like a "righteous messenger" and Matthew saying he is like a "wise philosopher;" right after Jesus had appointed James as the leader of the church after his death (*Thomas* 12).[100]

The Gospel of Simon account of this story is very much like *Thomas*, but instead has Thomas saying Jesus must be "a" (not "the") Son of God (*Simon* 19:1-6); a gnostic interpretation consistent throughout *Simon*, as also with the use of the word "Christ," which literally means anointed.[101] Interestingly, the related passages in the two other synoptic gospels have Peter using the word "Christ," not "the" Son of God - *Luke* 9:20 and *Mark* 8:29.

Without *Matthew* 16:18, the accepted gospels would have no part where Simon Peter is given the mandate as church leader. The legitimacy of the developing Catholic Church in Rome would be called into question.

The one time use of the name Simon Peter in *Luke* 5:8 provides an example of a revision by a likely *Thomas* sympathizer. The name usage links the previously discussed story of the miraculous catch of fish in *John* 21:1-22 to that of *Luke* 5:1-11. The distinguishable feature differences between the two in this case are that *Luke* has the story positioned with the selection of Simon Peter as an apostle, whereas *John* has it in conjunction with the discussion between Jesus and Simon Peter regarding the fate of the beloved disciple.

The other synoptic gospels do not include the story of the miraculous catch of fish, but do include the selection of Simon Peter as an apostle. In the case of *Luke* 5:8, Simon Peter is made to say to Jesus "Depart from me; for I am a sinful man, O Lord."

The implication is clear – Simon Peter is not worthy. The linkage is also clear – in *John* 21:20-22 Simon Peter questions Jesus as to what is to happen to the beloved disciple (i.e., Mary Magdalene) at the conclusion of the story of the miraculous catch – in *Thomas* 114 Simon Peter believes females (e.g., Mary Magdalene) are not worthy – in *Simon* 40:25-38 Simon Peter questions Jesus as to what is to happen to Mary Magdalene, Simon Peter believing females unworthy.

The Gospel of Simon clearly paints Simon Peter in a negative light. Rather than building a church upon the stone (i.e., rock) as *Matthew* 16:18 cites; Jesus warns Simon Peter on two occasions in *Simon* (19:9 and 32:2) not to be a stone upon which others stumble (*Matthew* 16:23 has a similar reference). Tradition claims that Simon Peter requested that he be crucified upside down because he believed himself unworthy to be crucified in the same manner as Jesus;[102] a differing interpretation could be that he knew that he had turned the teachings of Jesus upside down.

Of course, Simon Peter himself had only a small role in the evolving battle between what was to become the Catholic Church and the dissenting, Gnostic sects; although he set a tone and direction. Ultimately, he became a focal point for the forces that opposed a Gnostic interpretation of the ministry of Jesus. The church that ultimately evolved into the Roman Catholic Church claimed to follow the teachings and guidance of Simon Peter, who founded the See of Rome.

It is easy to see how Simon Peter would develop as a greater symbolic role than James. With James in Jerusalem, tending to the Jewish Christians and Simon Peter ministering, along with Paul, to Gentiles, it was inevitable that divergence would occur. The rapid growth of Christianity was among the Gentiles, not the Jewish people. Ultimately, the destruction of Jerusalem and the church's relationship with the Roman Empire cemented Simon Peter's symbolic status, leading the church away from Gnosticism as a political expedient.

The Role of Judas

Judas certainly has a reviled role in *The New Testament*, especially the synoptic gospels, where it is said that it would have been better if Judas had never been born (*Matthew* 26:24 and *Mark* 14:21). The recently recovered *Gospel of Judas* provides a vindication of the role of Judas, indicating that Judas did not betray Jesus; instead, his actions were those of obedience to the directions of Jesus.[103]

The Gospel of Simon is consistent with the *Gospel of Judas* in this more sympathetic treatment of Judas. A careful reading of *The Gospel of Simon* reveals plausible interpretations that Jesus directed his entry to Jerusalem (*Simon* 30:1) and the location of the Last Supper (*Simon* 34:2), as well as his own betrayal, with key phrases that were essentially passwords to cooperative acts between the stated individuals. During the Last Supper, Jesus states in *Simon* 34:25-26:

> 25 After supper, Jesus said, "I know whom I have chosen that the scripture may be fulfilled. He will be cursed for generations, yet he has sacrificed the most.
>
> 26 Now I tell you this before it comes; so that when it comes to pass, you may believe. Truly, I say to you, he that receives whomever I send receives me and he that receives me receives Him that sent me."

Furthermore, it is implied in *Simon* 29:4-6 that Jesus asked Judas to do something that the other disciples would find appalling (an interesting comparable situation can be found at *Thomas* 13).

John provides a somewhat more sympathetic portrayal of the role of Judas. *John* 13:18 indicates that Jesus chose Judas for the unhappy role of betrayal, although *The Gospel of Simon* goes further regarding Judas having sacrificed the most. The text clearly indicates that Jesus chose Judas for this onerous task. As stated by Jesus, the scripture could not have been fulfilled without Judas.

Jesus, the Savior – Sin vs. Suffering

One of the traditional concepts of Christianity is that belief in Jesus and his teachings will save one (deliverance or redemption) from the consequences of sin (God's wrath on Judgement Day).[104]

The Gospel of Simon presents a different way of viewing Jesus as Savior: belief and practice of the Truth taught by Jesus will result in being saved from suffering.

Suffering is seen as being caused by sin that comes from within men (*Simon* 17:1-7). Jesus proclaims that the Spirit he brings is not to cause suffering to men, but to save them from suffering (*Simon* 21:3-4).

One must be reborn of the Spirit (*Simon* 9:1-9), living the doctrine of Love and Truth as presented in the Sermon on the Mount (*Simon* 11:1-57); living in the moment, being not anxious for the future (*Simon* 11:41-47), nor tied to the past (*Simon* 14:6); following the way shown by Jesus (*Simon* 11:51-56).

Love is the highest principle (*Simon* 31:20-27). Jesus suffers the cross for Love (*Simon* 29:1); showing us that Love redeems the suffering caused by sin (*Simon* 19:13). Love for all is the law and the prophets (*Simon* 11:11-14). The Kingdom of God belongs to those that humble themselves (*Simon* 11:2) for Love (*Simon* 34:4-14).

The Naked Man

One of the more unusual passages in *The New Testament* is that contained in *Mark* 14:50-52, which describes a naked man after the arrest of Jesus at Gethsemane:

> 50 And they all forsook him, and fled.
>
> 51 And there followed him a certain young man, having a linen cloth cast about his naked body; and the young men laid hold on him:
>
> 52 And he left the linen cloth, and fled from them naked.

The meaning of this event has previously been considered obscure at best. That it appears in *Mark*, generally considered by academics as the oldest of the accepted gospels, makes it all the more fascinating.

Simon offers an illuminating interpretation. In *Simon* 20:4-5, the following scene is described.

> 4 Jesus called a little child unto him, set him in the midst of them, answering, "Truly, I say to you, unless you be born again and become as little children, you shall not enter into the Kingdom of Heaven.
>
> 5 Therefore, whoever shall humble himself as this little child, the same is greatest in the Kingdom of Heaven.

> When you disrobe like little children and tread on your garments, then you will find the Kingdom of Heaven.

Thomas 37 includes a somewhat similar statement.

> ... Jesus said, "When you strip off your clothes without being ashamed, and take your clothes and put them under your feet like little children and trample them, then you will see the Son of the Living One ...."

Simon 35:16-17 provides an alternative scene to *Mark* 14:50-52.

> 16 His disciples then forsook him and fled; but one followed closely behind Jesus, a certain young man, Simon, having a linen cloth wrapped about his body. An officer approached the young man to take him, but he cast his linen cloth to the ground; thereon he trampled the garment and fled from them naked.
>
> 17 Jesus then said, "Behold, a Son of God."

So here we have the lesson. The young man, likely Simon of *The Gospel of Simon*, has clearly heard the teachings of Jesus. His actions represent homage to Jesus in the Gnostic tradition; Jesus acknowledges the act, referring to the young man as a Son of God.

Further, this is consistent with the Garden of Eden story wherein Eve and Adam eat of the Tree of Knowledge, becoming as gods. As a result, they become ashamed of their nakedness and God casts them out of the garden. To return to Eden, to find the Kingdom of Heaven, one must be as a Child of God, unashamed of one's nakedness.

Who is Simon?

So, who is Simon of *The Gospel of Simon*? As generally agreed with the four accepted gospels, the true author is believed to be the namesake and/or authors that relied upon sources that were attributable to the gospels namesake. There is no reason to believe that *The Gospel of Simon* is any different.

While this does not answer the question of who Simon is, it is understood that this gospel would have been written sometime after the attributed source passed on their version of the gospel.

It is highly implausible that Simon Peter would be the attributed source given the text and the evolution of the church. Simon was a popular name during this period, so the possibilities are numerous.

There are two Simons referenced in *The Gospel of Simon* which are likely possibilities: Simon, one of the twelve disciples (*Simon* 7:1) and Simon, the brother of Jesus (*Simon* 13:2). The synoptic gospels agree that there was a disciple by the name of Simon (*Matthew* 10:4, *Mark* 3:18 and *Luke* 6:15) and a brother of Jesus called Simon (*Matthew* 13:55 and *Mark* 6:3).

Simon, the disciple, and Simon, the brother of Jesus, are both plausible candidates in that they would have had ready access to the secrets and mysteries of the teachings of Jesus. Given the scant mention of either and the lack of any lore surrounding them, it is difficult to make a convincing case for either as source or author, other than their proximity to Jesus.

Simon, the brother of Jesus, would probably be the more likely of the two. This hypothesis is predicated on the similarity of certain stories and parables between *The Gospel of Simon* and *The Gospel of Thomas*. Both books point to James, a brother of Jesus, as the first leader of the disciples after the death of Jesus.

Additionally, as previously discussed, authorship of *The Gospel of Thomas* has been attributed to Didymus Judas Thomas. Both the words "Didymus"[105] and "Thomas"[106] mean "twin" in Greek and Aramaic (Hebrew), respectively; in other words: Judas the Twin. *Simon* 13.2, *Matthew* 13:55 and *Mark* 6:3 all state that Jesus had a brother by the name of Judas. It has been a matter of conjecture as to whose twin brother Judas was, although Syrian Church tradition has Didymus Judas Thomas being the twin of Jesus.[107]

The three brothers, James, Thomas (also known as Judas), and Simon, actively involved in the ministry of Jesus would certainly make sense (*Simon* 7:1 states that Jesus started his ministry with his three brethren). All three names were identified as disciples and it is possible that Simon, the disciple, and Simon, the brother of Jesus, are one in the same.

The editor is of the opinion that Simon the disciple and Simon the brother of Jesus are, in fact, one in the same. Given their close proximity to Jesus, intimate knowledge of the secrets and mysteries, Simon, disciple and brother, would be in the best position to pass on or be the namesake for *The Gospel of Simon*.

Simon of Gitta

Nevertheless, an intriguing alternate candidate would be none other than Simon of Gitta. There are many stories in circulation attributed to Simon of Gitta, some of which are contradictory.

Simon of Gitta, otherwise pejoratively known as Simon Magus, is intriguing for a number of reasons, the first of which is the Magi or Magus connection. It would seem likely that Simon of Gitta was knowledgeable of the magi of the Zoroaster tradition.

The name Magus came to rest with Simon of Gitta primarily due to two sources of information, neither of which refers to him as Magus: *The Acts of the Apostles* [108] and the apocryphal *The Acts of Peter*.[109]

However both sources refer to him as using sorcery. Accordingly, it is understandable that over time the reference to sorcery, or magic, would evolve to the name Magus.

The Acts of the Apostles, 8:9-24, is the only canon biblical reference to Simon of Gitta. He is described as having a powerful influence over people in Samaria, having achieved it by bewitching the people with sorcery. The Samarian people are attributed as saying of Simon, "This man is the great power of God."

Nevertheless, he is converted and baptized as a Christian, becoming a follower of Philip upon hearing Philip preach concerning the Kingdom of God.

However, Simon runs afoul of Simon Peter when he attempts to buy the power of laying on of hands (Hence the term "simony," meaning attempting to buy or sell a thing of spiritual value. In *Simon* 14:2 Jesus forbids acceptance of payment for the Holy Soma.). Simon Peter condemns him as wicked and doomed. The reference to Simon ends with Simon asking Simon Peter to pray for his salvation.

Forgiveness is not given by Simon Peter. This is somewhat strange given the Christian philosophy of forgiveness, but is better understood when the relationship between Simon Peter and Simon is further explored.

Most of *The Acts of Peter* describes Simon Peter's confrontations with Simon in great detail. Reading the book leaves little doubt why it is considered apocryphal, but it does provide a clear and distinct overall impression of the relationship of the two.

In a nutshell, the book describes the two battling for the hearts, minds, and souls of the citizens of Rome. To the winner goes the spoils; in this case, Simon Peter and the Roman Catholic Church ultimately prevailed. Accordingly, Simon Peter et al write the history and description of what transpired.

Both lay claim to the power of God. What transpires, however, is not a thoughtful philosophical debate over various spiritual and religious tenets, but a battle over who can perform the greatest miracles.

Simon Peter commands dogs and infants to speak to the astonishment of Simon. Both raise the dead, but Simon Peter does so successfully, while Simon's relapse after exhibiting consciousness. Finally, Simon demonstrates his great power by flying above the citizens of Rome, while Simon Peter brings him crashing back to earth through the power of prayer, ultimately leading to Simon's death.

The conclusion to be drawn is that Simon Peter's faith and religious way is superior to that of Simon's. The accomplishments of Simon are branded sorcery, while those of Simon Peter are God given. The portion of the book addressing the relationship between the two ends describing Simon as the "angel of Satan."

Some things never change. When promoting one's beliefs, it is often useful to have an opponent that one can vilify, contrasting to one's own virtue. So it was in the early church, a number of competing visions of what Christianity was to become. Sects suppressed, especially the Gnostics, as power and religious interpretation coalesced around a common vision.

The Gnostic sect, the Simonians, developed around Simon of Gitta's teachings and lasted to the fourth century. Simon's doctrine was expressed in *The Great Declaration*, a mixture of Judaism and its variations at the time, including Christianity and Greek philosophy (according to Hippolytus of Rome in his refutation of heresies).[110]

The beliefs and practices of the Simonians would have put them in direct confrontation with the developing Roman Catholic Church. Their use of "libations" (possibly Soma) and philosophy of free love certainly accounts for the description of Simonians by Eusebius in circa AD 320 as:

> worshipping ... with incense, sacrifices and libations ....secret rites ... wonderstruck ... brim-full of frenzy and lunacy...of such a kind that not only can they not be put down in writing; they involve such appalling degradation, such unspeakable conduct, that no decent man would let a mention of them pass his lips ....[111]

Further, the Simonian philosophy that the divine existed in all, including women, and could be developed to an infinite state would be anathema to the early church. This philosophy would account for the fact that both Simon and his successor, Menander, considered themselves as having been sent by God.[112]

Casting himself as a Messiah, Christ, or Prophet would account for the early Catholic Church efforts to demonize and suppress his teachings, as well as the description by Eusebius that Simon was "the prime author of every heresy."

The Gospel of Simon would certainly be a heretical work given the evolution of the church. The use of entheogenic plants could easily be cast as sorcery.

However, while there are no significant, inherent conflicts between *The Gospel of Simon* and Simonian philosophy, there is very little usage of the philosophical terms that characterized the Simonians. Nevertheless, Simon of Gitta remains an interesting possibility as an inspiration for *The Gospel of Simon*, as he has been cast as the primary author of all heresies, Gnosticism included.[113]

Date of *The Gospel of Simon*

The other unanswered question regarding *The Gospel of Simon* is the date when it was written. Clearly the events are those circa 7 BC to AD 33. However, there is no physical evidence of any sort to establish it as based on an ancient text.

As discussed in the Preface, the English text found is likely circa 1970's. Accompanying notes referencing a predecessor Greek text are indicative of a much earlier source, however that evidence is not available. One can hope that publication of *The Gospel of Simon* will lead to the surfacing of any predecessor, original texts that may exist.

Conclusions

The Gospel of Simon presents a Gnostic vision of Christianity that proclaims that anyone can become a divine Child (Son or Daughter) of God – Christ like. While this was certainly a blasphemy during the time of Jesus, in today's society, especially those inclined towards New Age religions, such beliefs are no longer considered as radical.

The moral code presented is almost identical to traditional Christianity. However, *Simon* emphasizes being "saved" from "suffering," as opposed to being "saved" from "sin." Sin is seen as a cause of suffering; Jesus teaches us that Love redeems the suffering caused by sin.

Many questions ultimately remain unanswered. Did the original Christians really use entheogens? What is the source of the Holy Soma? Where did *The Gospel of Simon* come from?

Perhaps the most intriguing question is which of the early Christian sects was, in fact, the heresy? Were the Gnostics or the developing Catholic Church the heretics? For what reasons would a Christian sect align itself with the Roman Empire; and then proceed to suppress the other Christian sects, seeking to destroy all written evidence of their beliefs and practices?

Barring some disclosure by the current Roman Catholic Church, it seems unlikely that the answers to most of these questions will ever be known with certainty.

Regardless, *The Gospel of Simon* is a known work expressing a Gnostic, Christian perspective of the ministry of Jesus. Whether a work of early Christianity, a current revelation or fiction, the ultimate question is what truths are contained within.

EXHIBIT 1

FORGED INSCRIPTION IN A 1970 FIRST PRINTING OF *THE SACRED MUSHROOM AND THE CROSS*

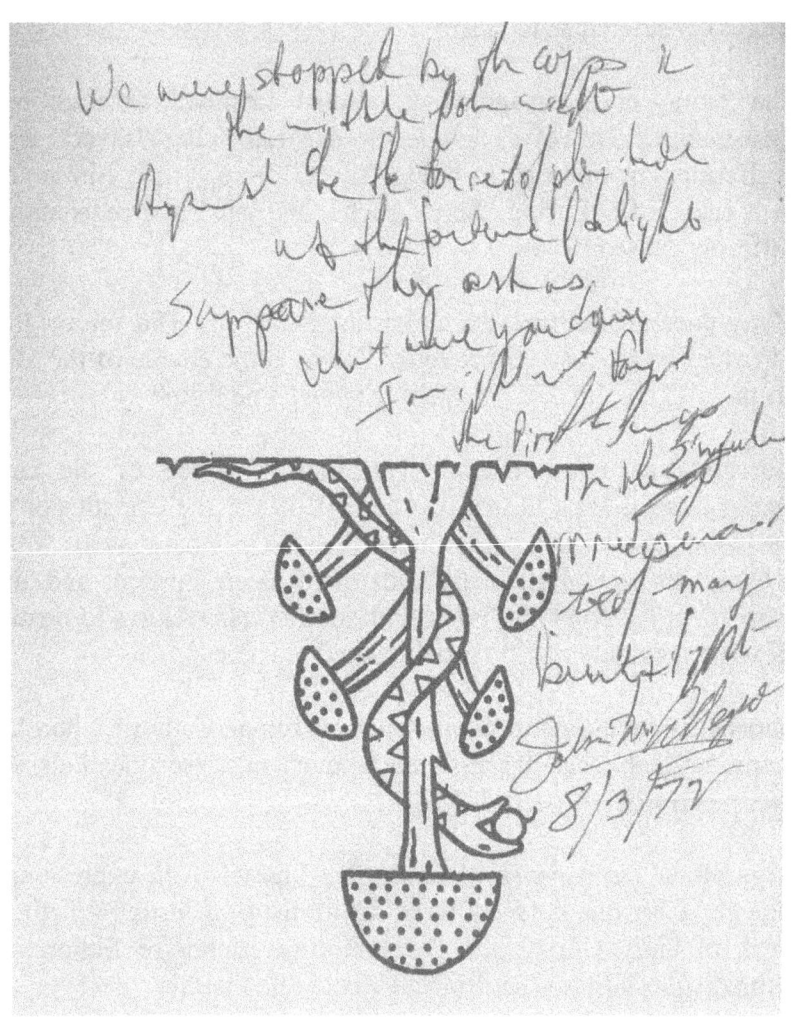

EXHIBIT 2

INTERPRETATION OF FORGED INSCRIPTION IN A 1970 FIRST PRINTING OF *THE SACRED MUSHROOM AND THE CROSS*

"We were stopped by the cops in
the middle of the night
Highest be the torrent of plenitude
of the fortune of delight
Suppose they ask us
What were you doing
I might not [un-interpreted]
I'm first to [un-interpreted]
[un-interpreted line]
iridescence
[un-interpreted] of [un-interpreted]
beauty & light

John M. Allegro
8/3/72"

Interpretations from readers are gratefully accepted. Contributors of interpretive input do so without compensation of any kind. Interpretations may be e-mailed to:

editor@SunshinePublishingOfClearwater.com

REFERENCE NOTES

Preface

1. James M. Robinson (General Editor), *The Nag Hammadi Library* (Harper & Row, 1978), pgs. 10 and 21-22.

2. Robinson, *Nag Hammadi*, pg. 2.

3. Richard Valantasis, *The Gospel of Thomas* (Routledge, 1997), pg. 12.

4. Robinson, *Nag Hammadi*, pg. 23.

5. Robinson, *Nag Hammadi*.

6. Geza Vermes, *The Dead Sea Scrolls. Qumran in Perspective* (Collins, 1977), pg. 15.

7. Robert H. Eisenman, *James, the Brother of Jesus: The Key to Unlocking the Secrets of Early Christianity and the Dead Sea Scrolls* (Viking, 1997).

8. John M. Allegro, *The Dead Sea Scrolls and the Christian Myth* (Westbridge Books, 1979).

9. John C. Trever, *The Dead Sea Scrolls* (Gorgias Press LLC, 2003).

10. Judith A. Brown, *John Marco Allegro: The Maverick of the Dead Sea Scrolls* (Wm. B. Eerdmans Publishing Co., 2005), pg. 26.

11. Brown, *Allegro: The Maverick*, pgs. 157-158.

12. Brown, *Allegro: The Maverick*, pgs. 174-184.

13. Brown, *Allegro: The Maverick*, pg. 273.

14. John M. Allegro, *The Sacred Mushroom and the Cross* (Hodder and Stoughton, 1970).

15. Allegro, *The Sacred Mushroom*, pgs. xiv-xv.

16. Allegro, *The Sacred Mushroom*, pg. xx.

17. Sidnie White Crawford, "Review of Judith Anne Brown, John Marco Allegro: The Maverick of the Dead Sea Scrolls," *Catholic Biblical Quarterly* 68, 4 (2006): pg. 725.

18. Michael Hoffman, "Wasson and Allegro on the Tree of Knowledge as Amanita," *Journal of Higher Criticism* (2006).

19. John A. Rush, *Failed God: Fractured Myth in a Fragile World* (Frog Books, 2008).

20. Allegro, *The Sacred Mushroom*, pg. xxi.

21. Robinson, *Nag Hammadi*, pgs. 3-10.

22. David Brakke, *The Gnostics: Myth, Ritual, and Diversity in Early Christianity* (Harvard University Press, 2012), pgs. ix-x.

23. Samuel Angus, *The Mystery-Religions and Christianity: A Study in the Religious Background of Early Christianity* (Dover Publications, 2011), pg. 54.

24. Elaine Pagels, *Beyond Belief: The Secret Gospel of Thomas* (Random House, 2003), pgs. 170-183.

25. "The New Testament of Our Lord and Saviour Jesus Christ," *Holy Bible, King James Version, Family Reference Edition* (Thomas Nelson Publishers, 1971), pgs. 817-1084.

26. Pagels, *Beyond Belief*, pg. 177.

27. Elaine Pagels and Karen L. King, *Reading Judas: The Gospel of Judas and the Shaping of Christianity* (Viking Adult, 2007).

28. Irenaeus of Lyons, "Against the Heresies," *Ante-Nicene Fathers: Volume I: The Apostolic Fathers, Justin Martyr,*

Irenaeus, Translators Alexander Roberts and James Donaldson (Wm. B. Eerdmans Publishing Company, 1950).

29. James M. Robinson, *The Secrets of Judas: The Story of the Misunderstood Disciple and His Lost Gospel* (Harper, 2006), pg. 183.

30. Irenaeus of Lyons, "Against the Heresies," Book 1, Ch. XXXI.1.

Analysis

31. "The New Testament," *Holy Bible*, pgs. 817-934.

32. Stephen L. Harris, *Understanding the Bible* (Mayfield, 1985).

33. "The Gospel according to St. Mark," *Holy Bible*, 1:1-16:20.

34. "The Gospel according to St. Matthew," *Holy Bible*, 1:1-28:20.

35. "The Gospel according to St. Luke," *Holy Bible*, 1:1-24:53.

36. "The Gospel according to St. John," *Holy Bible*, 1:1-21:25.

37. John S. Kloppenborg, *Q, the Earliest Gospel: An Introduction to the Original Stories and Sayings of Jesus* (Westminster John Knox Press, 2008).

38. Marvin Meyer (Translator), "The Gospel of Thomas," in *Beyond Belief: The Secret Gospel of Thomas* by Elaine Pagels (Random House, 2003), pgs. 227-242 (1 to 114).

39. Walter Bauer, *Orthodoxy and Heresy in Earliest Christianity* (Sigler Press, 1996).

40. Robinson, *Nag Hammadi*, pgs. 1-10.

41. Antoine Faivre, *Theosophy, Imagination, Tradition: Studies in Western Esotericism*, Translated by Christine Rhone (State University of New York Press, 2000), pgs. 7-8.

42. Bauer, *Orthodoxy and Heresy*.

43. Elaine Pagels, *The Gnostic Gospels* (Vintage, 1989).

44. Pagels, *Beyond Belief*, pgs. 173-174.

45. Brown, *Allegro: The Maverick*, pgs. 270-272.

46. H. Nyberg, "Religious use of Hallucinogenic Fungi: A Comparison between Siberian and Mesoamerican Cultures," *Karstenia* 32 (1992): pgs. 71–80.

47. Hong-En Jiang, Xiao Li, You-Xing Zhao, David K. Ferguson, Francis Hueber, Subir Bera, Yu-Fei Wang, Liang-Cheng Zhao, Chang-Jiang Liu, and Cheng-Sen Li, "A New Insight into Cannabis Sativa (Cannabaceae) Utilization from 2500-year-old Yanghai Tombs, Xinjiang, China," *Journal of Ethnopharmacology* 108, 3 (2006): pgs. 414–422.

48. Edward M. Brecher and the Editors of Consumer Reports, *Licit & Illicit Drugs*, (Consumers Union of United States Inc., 1972), pgs. 337-345 and 397-402.

49. R. Gordon Wasson, Albert Hofmann, and Carl A. P. Ruck, *The Road to Eleusis: Unveiling the Secret of the Mysteries* (North Atlantic Books, 2008).

50. Richard Evan Schultes, "Hallucinogens of Plant Origin," *Science* 163 (January 17, 1969): pgs. 251-252.

51. Thomas Szasz, *Ceremonial Chemistry* (Learning Publications Inc., 1985).

52. Allegro, *The Sacred Mushroom*.

53. David York, "Famous Scholar Challenges the Faith of Centuries: Christ and the Sacred Mushroom," *Sunday Mirror*, February 15, 1970, pg. 1.

54. Hoffman, "Wasson and Allegro on the Tree of Knowledge as Amanita."

55. Rush, *Failed God: Fractured Myth in a Fragile World.*

56. "The Old Testament," *Holy Bible, King James Version, Family Reference Edition* (Thomas Nelson Publishers, 1971), pgs. 1-813.

57. Allegro, *The Sacred Mushroom*, pgs. 36-37 and 40.

58. John Lust, "Mandrake," *The Herb Book* (Bantam Books, 1974), pg. 264.

59. John Ramsbottom, *Mushrooms and Toadstools: A Study of the Activities of Fungi* (Collins, 1953), pgs. 34-35.

60. Allegro, *The Sacred Mushroom*, pg. 80.

61. Wasson, Hofmann, and Ruck, *The Road to Eleusis*.

62. Josephus, *Jewish Antiquities*, Translator Ralph Marcus (Harvard University Press, 1937), Book XI, Chapter 8.5.

63. Wasson, Hofmann, and Ruck, *The Road to Eleusis*, pgs. 85-136.

64. Blaise Danny Staples (Translator), "The Homeric Hymn to Demeter" in *The Road to Eleusis* by Wasson, Hofmann, and Ruck (North Atlantic Books, 2008), pgs. 69-83.

65. Staples, "The Homeric Hymn to Demeter," pg. 74.

66. Stephen E. Jones, *Secrets of Time* (God's Kingdom Ministries, 1996).

67. Torsten Passie, John H. Halpern, Dirk O. Stichtenoth, Hinderk M. Emrich and Annelie Hintzen, "The Pharmacology of Lysergic Acid Diethylamide: A Review," *CNS Neuroscience & Therapeutics*, 14 (2008): pgs. 295–314.

68. Passie and others, "The Pharmacology of Lysergic Acid Diethylamide: A Review."

69. Ken R. Vincent, *The Magi: From Zoroaster to the "Three Wise Men"* (Bibal Pr., 1999).

70. Dieter Taillieu and Mary Boyce, *Encyclopaedia Iranica* (Mazda Publications, 2002), "Haoma."

71. Wendy Doniger O'Flaherty (Translator), *The Rig Veda* (Penguin Books, 1981).

72. Thomas Oberlies, *Der Rigveda und seine Religion* (Insel Verlag GmbH, 2012), pg. 158.

73. Jan E. M. Houben, "The Soma-Haoma Problem," *Electronic Journal of Vedic Studies*, May 4, 2003, 9/1a.

74. R. Gordon Wasson, *Soma: Divine Mushroom of Immortality* (Harcourt Brace Jovanovich, 1972).

75. Allegro, *The Sacred Mushroom*, pg. 39.

76. Wasson, Hofmann, and Ruck, *The Road to Eleusis*, pg. 91.

77. Carl A. P. Ruck, *Sacred Mushrooms of the Goddess: Secrets of Eleusis* (Ronin Publishing, Inc., 2006), pg. 19.

78. Chris Bennett, *Cannabis and the Soma Solution* (Trine Day, 2010).

79. Houben, "The Soma-Haoma Problem."

80. Terence McKenna, *Food of the Gods: The Search for the Original Tree of Knowledge, a Radical History of Plants, Drugs, and Human Evolution* (Bantam, 1993).

81. Ralph T. H. Griffith (Translator), *The Rig Veda* (Forgotten Books, 2008).

82. Jean L. McKichnie (Editor), *Webster's New Twentieth Century Dictionary* (Simon & Schuster, 1979), "Soma" pgs. 1728-1729.

83. W. Y Evans-Wentz (Translator), *The Tibetan Book of the Dead* (Oxford University Press, 1927).

84. Timothy Leary, Ph.D., Ralph Metzner, Ph.D., and Richard Alpert, Ph.D., *The Psychedelic Experience: A Manual Based on the Tibetan Book of the Dead* (The Citadel Press, 1964).

85. Pagels, *Beyond Belief*.

86. Mark Allan Powell, *Jesus as a Figure in History: How Modern Historians View the Man from Galilee* (Westminster John Knox Press, 1998), pg. 43.

87. Chris Keith, "Recent and Previous Research on the Pericope Adulterae (John 7.53—8.11)," *Currents in Biblical Research* 6, 3 (2008): pgs. 377–404.

88. Bruce M. Metzger, *A Textual Commentary on the Greek New Testament* (Hendrickson Publishers, 2005), pgs 187-189.

89. Eusebius, *The History of the Church*, Translator G. A. Williamson (Dorset Press, 1965), Book 3.39, pg. 153.

90. Eusebius, *History*, Appendix F, pg. 424.

91. Moses Stuart, *A Commentary on the Apocalypse, Volume I* (Allen, Morrill and Wardell, 1845), pgs. 339-344.

92. Eusebius, *History*, Book 2.25, pgs. 104-105; Book 3.28, pgs. 137-139; Book 6.20, pg. 261.

93. Valantasis, *The Gospel of Thomas*, pg. 12.

94. Meyer, "The Gospel of Thomas," pgs. 241-242 (*Thomas* 114).

95. Robinson, *Nag Hammadi*.

96. James Owen, "Papyrus Reveals New Clues to Ancient World," *National Geographic News*, April 25, 2005.

97. D. R. Hillers, "Revelation 13:18 and a Scroll from Murabba'at," *Bulletin of the American Schools of Oriental Research* 170 (1963): pg. 65.

98. Margaret Starbird, *Magdalene's Lost Legacy: Symbolic Numbers and the Sacred Union in Christianity* (Bear & Company, 2003), pgs. 49 and 139.

99. Eusebius, *History*, Book 2.1, pg. 72.

100. Meyer, "The Gospel of Thomas," pgs. 228-229 (*Thomas* 12-13).

101. McKichnie, *Webster's*, "Christ" pg.320.

102. Granger Ryan and Helmut Ripperger (Translators), *The Golden Legend of Jacobus De Voragine, Part One* (Longmans, Green and Co., 1941).

103. Pagels and King, *The Gospel of Judas*.

104. Bruce Demarest, *The Cross and Salvation: The Doctrine of Salvation* (Crossway, 2006).

105. McKichnie, *Webster's*, "Didymous," pg. 507.

106. McKichnie, *Webster's*, "Thomas," pg. 1899.

107. Helmut Koester, "Introduction to The Gospel of Thomas," Robinson, *Nag Hammadi*, pg. 117.

108. "The Acts of the Apostles," *Holy Bible*, 1:1-28:31.

109. M. R. James (Translator), "The Acts of Peter," *The Apocryphal New Testament* (Clarendon Press, 1924).

110. Hippolytus of Rome, *The Refutation of all Heresies*, Translator F. Legge (The MacMillan Company, 1921), Books IV and VI.

111. Eusebius, *History*, Book 2.13, pg. 87.

112. Gerard van Groningen, *First Century Gnosticism: Its Origin and Motifs* (E. J. Brill, 1967).

113. Eusebius, *History*, Book 2.13, pg. 86.

BIBLIOGRAPHY

Allegro, John M. *The Dead Sea Scrolls and the Christian Myth.* Westbridge Books, 1979.

Allegro, John M. *The Sacred Mushroom and the Cross.* Hodder and Stoughton, 1970.

Angus, Samuel. *The Mystery-Religions and Christianity: A Study in the Religious Background of Early Christianity.* Dover Publications, 2011.

Bauer, Walter. *Orthodoxy and Heresy in Earliest Christianity.* Sigler Press, 1996.

Bennett, Chris. *Cannabis and the Soma Solution.* Trine Day, 2010.

Brakke, David. *The Gnostics: Myth, Ritual, and Diversity in Early Christianity.* Harvard University Press, 2012.

Brecher, Edward M. and the Editors of Consumer Reports. *Licit & Illicit Drugs.* Consumers Union of United States Inc., 1972.

Brown, Judith A. *John Marco Allegro: The Maverick of the Dead Sea Scrolls.* Wm. B. Eerdmans Publishing Co., 2005.

Crawford, Sidnie White. "Review of Judith Anne Brown, John Marco Allegro: The Maverick of the Dead Sea Scrolls." *Catholic Biblical Quarterly* 68, 4 (2006).

Demarest, Bruce. *The Cross and Salvation: The Doctrine of Salvation.* Crossway, 2006.

Eisenman, Robert H. *James, the Brother of Jesus: The Key to Unlocking the Secrets of Early Christianity and the Dead Sea Scrolls*. Viking, 1997.

Eusebius. *The History of the Church*. Translated by G. A. Williamson. Dorset Press, 1965.

Evans-Wentz, W. Y. (Translator). *The Tibetan Book of the Dead*. Oxford University Press, 1927.

Faivre, Antoine. *Theosophy, Imagination, Tradition: Studies in Western Esotericism*. Translated by Christine Rhone. State University of New York Press, 2000.

Griffith, Ralph T. H. (Translator). *The Rig Veda*. Forgotten Books, 2008.

Groningen, Gerald van. *First Century Gnosticism: Its Origin and Motifs*. E. J. Brill, 1967.

Harris, Stephen L. *Understanding the Bible*. Mayfield, 1985.

Hillers, D. R. "Revelation 13:18 and a Scroll from Murabba'at." *Bulletin of the American Schools of Oriental Research* 170 (1963).

Hippolytus of Rome. *The Refutation of all Heresies*. Translated by F. Legge. The MacMillan Company, 1921.

Hoffman, Michael. "Wasson and Allegro on the Tree of Knowledge as Amanita." *Journal of Higher Criticism* (2006).

Holy Bible, King James Version, Family Reference Edition. Thomas Nelson Publishers, 1971.

Houben, Jan E. M. "The Soma-Haoma Problem." *Electronic Journal of Vedic Studies* (May 4, 2003).

Irenaeus of Lyons. "Against the Heresies" in *Ante-Nicene Fathers: Volume I: The Apostolic Fathers, Justin Martyr, Irenaeus*. Translated by Alexander Roberts and James Donaldson. Wm. B. Eerdmans Publishing Company, 1950.

James, M. R. (Translator). "The Acts of Peter" in *The Apocryphal New Testament*. Clarendon Press, 1924.

Jiang, Hong-En, Xiao Li, You-Xing Zhao, David K. Ferguson, Francis Hueber, Subir Bera, Yu-Fei Wang, Liang-Cheng Zhao, Chang-Jiang Liu, and Cheng-Sen Li. "A New Insight into Cannabis Sativa (Cannabaceae) Utilization from 2500-year-old Yanghai Tombs, Xinjiang, China." *Journal of Ethnopharmacology* 108, 3 (2006).

Jones, Stephen E. *Secrets of Time*. God's Kingdom Ministries, 1996.

Josephus. *Jewish Antiquities*. Translated by Ralph Marcus. Harvard University Press, 1937.

Keith, Chris. "Recent and Previous Research on the Pericope Adulterae (John 7.53—8.11)." *Currents in Biblical Research* 6, 3 (2008).

Kloppenborg, John S. *Q, the Earliest Gospel: An Introduction to the Original Stories and Sayings of Jesus*. Westminster John Knox Press, 2008.

Koester, Helmut. "Introduction to The Gospel of Thomas" in *The Nag Hammadi Library*. General Editor James M. Robinson. Harper & Row, 1978.

Leary, Timothy, Ph.D., Ralph Metzner, Ph.D., and Richard Alpert, Ph.D. *The Psychedelic Experience: A Manual Based on the Tibetan Book of the Dead*. The Citadel Press, 1964.

Lust, John. *The Herb Book*. Bantam Books, 1974.

McKenna, Terence. *Food of the Gods: The Search for the Original Tree of Knowledge, a Radical History of Plants, Drugs, and Human Evolution*. Bantam, 1993.

McKichnie, Jean L. (Editor). *Webster's New Twentieth Century Dictionary*. Simon & Schuster, 1979.

Metzger, Bruce M. *A Textual Commentary on the Greek New Testament*. Hendrickson Publishers, 2005.

Meyer, Marvin (Translator). "The Gospel of Thomas" in *Beyond Belief: The Secret Gospel of Thomas* by Elaine Pagels. Random House, 2003.

Nyberg, H. "Religious use of Hallucinogenic Fungi: A Comparison between Siberian and Mesoamerican Cultures." *Karstenia* 32 (1992).

Oberlies, Thomas. *Der Rigveda und seine Religion*. Insel Verlag GmbH, 2012.

O'Flaherty, Wendy Doniger (Translator). *The Rig Veda*. Penguin Books, 1981.

Owen, James. "Papyrus Reveals New Clues to Ancient World." *National Geographic News* (April 25, 2005).

Pagels, Elaine. *Beyond Belief: The Secret Gospel of Thomas*. Random House, 2003.

Pagels, Elaine. *The Gnostic Gospels*. Vintage, 1989.

Pagels, Elaine and Karen L. King. *Reading Judas: The Gospel of Judas and the Shaping of Christianity*. Viking Adult, 2007.

Passie, Torsten, John H. Halpern, Dirk O. Stichtenoth, Hinderk M. Emrich and Annelie Hintzen. "The Pharmacology of Lysergic Acid Diethylamide: A Review." *CNS Neuroscience & Therapeutics* 14 (2008).

Powell, Mark Allan. *Jesus as a Figure in History: How Modern Historians View the Man from Galilee*. Westminster John Knox Press, 1998.

Ramsbottom, John. *Mushrooms and Toadstools: A Study of the Activities of Fungi*. Collins, 1953.

Robinson, James M. (General Editor). *The Nag Hammadi Library*. Harper & Row, 1978.

Robinson, James M. *The Secrets of Judas: The Story of the Misunderstood Disciple and His Lost Gospel*. Harper, 2006.

Ruck, Carl A. P. *Sacred Mushrooms of the Goddess: Secrets of Eleusis*. Ronin Publishing, Inc., 2006.

Rush, John A. *Failed God: Fractured Myth in a Fragile World*. Frog Books, 2008.

Ryan, Granger, and Helmut Ripperger (Translators). *The Golden Legend of Jacobus De Voragine, Part One*. Longmans, Green and Co., 1941.

Schultes, Richard Evan. "Hallucinogens of Plant Origin." *Science* 163 (January 17, 1969).

Staples, Blaise Danny (Translator). "The Homeric Hymn to Demeter" in *The Road to Eleusis* by R. Gordon Wasson, Albert Hofmann, and Carl A. P. Ruck. North Atlantic Books, 2008.

Starbird, Margaret. *Magdalene's Lost Legacy: Symbolic Numbers and the Sacred Union in Christianity*. Bear & Company, 2003.

Stuart, Moses. *A Commentary on the Apocalypse, Volume I.* Allen, Morrill and Wardell, 1845.

Szasz, Thomas. *Ceremonial Chemistry.* Learning Publications Inc., 1985.

Taillieu, Dieter and Mary Boyce. *Encyclopaedia Iranica.* Mazda Publications, 2002.

Trever, John C. *The Dead Sea Scrolls.* Gorgias Press LLC, 2003.

Valantasis, Richard. *The Gospel of Thomas.* Routledge, 1997.

Vermes, Geza. *The Dead Sea Scrolls. Qumran in Perspective.* Collins, 1977.

Vincent, Ken R. *The Magi: From Zoroaster to the "Three Wise Men."* Bibal Pr., 1999.

Wasson, R. Gordon, Albert Hofmann, and Carl A. P. Ruck. *The Road to Eleusis: Unveiling the Secret of the Mysteries.* North Atlantic Books, 2008.

Wasson, R. Gordon. *Soma: Divine Mushroom of Immortality.* Harcourt Brace Jovanovich, 1972.

York, David. "Famous Scholar Challenges the Faith of Centuries: Christ and the Sacred Mushroom." *Sunday Mirror*, February 15, 1970, pg. 1.

Also by Christopher Carpenter

Orange Sunshine and the Psychedelic Sunrise

www.ingramcontent.com/pod-product-compliance
Lightning Source LLC
LaVergne TN
LVHW041628070426
835507LV00008B/508